CW01646698

Dandelions

This revised expanded edition with a foreword by Catherine Burgass
Published 2025 by Barewall Books
2–4 Market Place, The White House, Burslem, Stoke-on-Trent ST6 4AT.

First published 1993, printed by Newcastle Instant Print.

Re-issued 2007 by Henson Editorial and North Staffordshire Press with a foreword by Peter Cheeseman.

Re-issued 2015 by Henson Editorial Services and North Staffordshire Press with a foreword by Ray Johnson and Catherine Burgass.

This revised expanded edition © The Estate of Arthur Berry 2025.

Designed by Jason Conway – The Daydream Academy.

Editorial by Jane Wood.

Paintings by Arthur Berry
Front cover and p.183: *Dandelions* (1969)
p.3: Cover drawing for *Dandelions* 1st edition (c.1993)
p.35: *The Chain Row* (1994)
p.49: *Shanghai Lil* (1993)
p.171: *The Blossom Blown* (c.1990s)
p.186: *The Good Son* (1973)

Back cover: Photo by Gerald Wells, Northern Photographers (1984)

A catalogue record of this book is available from the British Library.

ISBN 978-1-83654-522-4

Printed and bound by Tradeprint Distribution Limited using paper that originated from sustainable sources comprising of FSC and PEFC PFSE paper stocks.

Barewall Books is a brand name of Barewall Ltd.

This commemorative edition has been produced as part of **Arthur Berry 100**, a project commemorating the centenary of the birth of Arthur Berry, made possible with The National Lottery Heritage Fund. Thanks to National Lottery players, we have been able to produce this extended new edition of *Dandelions*.

DANDELIONS

POEMS

Arthur Berry

bare
WALL

For Cynth

Contents

Introduction to the first edition

These poems were written a few years ago. On reading them recently I could see more clearly than I did then the themes that ran through them: the streets of my early childhood, the moorland landscape, the pit villages, public houses, chip shops, night town and later avenue life were all strands in the work. Also running through them is the inexorable fact of time and change.

It was a long time before I noticed change enough to take a serious note of it, but it began to seep in when people I knew died and weren't there any more. This was in the late twenties and thirties. Then came the fracture of the war and overnight the world became a bigger place, lives were uprooted and life became much more exciting – that is, if you weren't bombed or bayoneted, drowned or starved to death.

Then immediately after the war there was an optimism in the land. Things were going to change and change they did. The old mangle rollers were replaced by rubber wringers, the iron grates by little fancy tiled affairs, and the elegant, slim paper packets of five Woodbines disappeared, as did the idle men and the dole men who stood at street corners, and a world of welfare took their place. Streets were demolished, new council estates sprang up around the perimeters of the city. There were categories for everyone's particular circumstances, that is, if you knew how to fill the forms in. There were smokeless zones and pills for every ailment. It was an electronic world where none of the wires showed, and on the face of it, a better world for ordinary people. But as usual there was a price to pay. The values that had held the working class together began to slowly be eroded. The sons no longer had either the stoicism or wit of their fathers. They chose a different style, as there were now many styles to choose from. There was loud music everywhere, and at night there were screams in the streets and everywhere innocence was attacked. The old had to bolt their doors at night, the favourite expression of the youths was a snarl and down the backs among the dandelions there were smashed bottles and empty cans of glue.

This then is a rough account of the times I have lived in, and I recognise it as the main theme of most of my work. I did not consciously think about it at the time, as I wrote my poems, but it must have seeped in – as did various bits of daft, thank goodness.

Arthur Berry, 1993.

Foreword to the centenary edition

Looking back in 1984, Arthur Berry wrote: 'it is the richness of poor things that I am drawn to. The dandelion is my true flower and my greatest loss is that this world I love is disappearing'. The dandelion, as most gardeners know, is a persistent weed by virtue of a taproot from which it can regenerate. It does have symbolic value as a bitter herb and some poetic representation, most notably in Walt Whitman's 'The First Dandelion'. However, it is quite unlike the lily or the rose, with their high cultural and horticultural status, and is known by a particularly vulgar name after its diuretic effect. But this 'sour yellow' 'rag sun' of a flower, '[f]ed on the dried excrement of dogs', speaks of the artist's own deep-rooted identity in the working-class culture of the pottery towns and mining villages of North Staffordshire.

Arthur Berry was born in the village of Smallthorne *with* the city of Stoke-on-Trent in 1925. Stoke's six towns were not so much unified as cobbled together – each town 'an argument of streets', collectively a 'world of codge'. The manifest principle of making do has been noted by numerous commentators, including 'Five Towns' novelist Arnold Bennett. Unlike Bennett, who left the 'slovenly makeshift' of the Potteries at the earliest opportunity, Arthur declared himself happiest in this world of codge and stuck close to home most of his life.

As the child of a solidly working-class family, Arthur's career as an artist could not have been predicted. However, the paralysis of his right arm in infancy rendered him unfit for manual work and luckily his talent for drawing was spotted. He was enrolled as a junior at the Burslem Art School and from there, following an unsuccessful trial as a pottery painter, to the Royal College of Art.

Arthur clearly had a love of language and feeling for literature, even his neuroses had a poetic bent: 'I had always been seduced by the sensuality of words and my mind was regularly the prisoner of some mad ditty which I'd be compulsed to repeat thousands of times till I'd worn it out.' But, as ever for Arthur there was a stumbling block, and in this case it was the lack of a formal literary education.

Literary influences are briefly discussed in the Introduction to *On the Street* and mentioned at times in his memoir: Ezra Pound, 'T.S. Eliot, C. Day Lewis and Stephen Spender, and particularly the surrealist poets'. It was Eliot who counselled in his 1919 essay 'Tradition and the Individual Talent', that the modern poet should have 'a feeling that the whole of the literature of Europe from Homer has a simultaneous existence'. Arthur found the giants at his shoulder oppressive and turned away:

> I soon realised that the poets I admired were all very highly educated men to start with, whereas I was a comparative hayseed and that if I was to write anything of value, it had to be about the world in my head and not the world in somebody else's.

In spite of these protestations, Eliot continued to hover over his work and the 1993 cover design of *Dandelions* was in shameless imitation of the prestigious publisher Faber & Faber's volumes of the time. Their starry backlist included Philip Larkin, Spender, Pound and Eliot. Arthur had a troubled relationship with canonical literature akin to his relationship with the European tradition in art. He felt unduly influenced and at the same time inadequate in his struggles developing subject and technique.

There are some local poets who might have helped. They include Noah Heath, a working potter, who seized on his Sunday-school education to produce two volumes of *Miscellaneous Poems* in the early nineteenth century. These poems feature the locality and its 'low' pursuits as bull-baiting. A later nineteenth-century poet, William Steele, also wrote of local events, often comically and in dialect. Neither Heath nor Steele (both dubbed Potteries poets), are mentioned in Arthur's published work, but a photocopy of Steele's *Writings in Prose and Rhyme* has been found in his effects.

Contemporary voices that resonate with Arthur's include that of dour Midlander Larkin (who also shared Arthur's pronounced morbid streak) in the melancholic tone of poems such as 'As Bad as a Mile' in *Whitsun Weddings* (1964). Also relevant – though little touted abroad – is a significant Stoke corpus generated in Berry's era. This body of work (not a movement as such), was effectively spearheaded by distinguished poet Charles Tomlinson. The first of Tomlinson's Stoke poems, 'The Slag Heap', was published in 1950 and Stoke continued to feature significantly in subsequent collections including *The Way In* (1974). Here the title poem contains a familiar scene: 'A century's lath and rafters. Bulldozers/ Gobble a street up.' Another notable Stoke author was John Wain, author of several Stoke poems, including (part of) *Letters to Five Artists* (1969) and *Mid-week Period Return: Home Thoughts of a Native* (1982), along with a Stoke-set novel published in 1958. Berry's fellow Burslem boys, John Shelton and Jack Simcock, also produced slim volumes of poetry, in 1974 and 1975 respectively. All this is to say, that while Arthur was evidently one to plough his own furrow, he was not unique as a poet of this place, at this time.

Arthur started writing poetry seriously around 1970, by his own account to give the characters of his paintings a voice, but *Dandelions* has a slightly obscure genesis. In 1978 Arthur was asked on the *ATV Today* local news programme why none of the hundreds of poems he had written had ever been published. In response, he referred enigmatically to a curious pattern of circumstances that had led to his light being hidden under a particularly large bushel. On the eventual publication of *Dandelions* he is quoted in the *Evening Sentinel* as saying, "Ten years ago I wrote about 200 poems", "over a period of two to two and a half years". In fact 18 poems, including a version of 'Dandelions', had already been published in a small print run of *Poems* (1972), while a more substantial volume, *Street Corner Ballads*, was produced by Ironmarket Press in 1977. Poems in the *Dandelions* typescript (a looseleaf folder) are sporadically dated between 1970 and 1981. Such inconsistencies suggest, perhaps, that Arthur was happy to capitalise on a good story – even his memoir is advertised as a 'novel'. Though a potential headache for any future biographer, this need not trouble the reader of the poems to the extent that they convey something true.

To the poems: modern life is excoriated – there is nothing positive in the whole volume. 'The Bulldozers' gobble up entire communities and the youth have turned into violent 'gob-eyed loons'. The fabric of this brave new world is hard-edged or shoddy ('Concrete Blocks'), its splendours such as polished aluminium toilet fittings or 'a telephone kiosk made in the shape of a plastic dome' in 'A Fly in the Ointment' are specious and ridiculous. This contrasts with the classic dignity of the old, even to 'The Gentlemen's Convenience'. Modern institutions are faceless and their Kafkaesque systems diminish precisely those they purport to help in 'Welfare State Blues': 'Down the corridors of the powerless/ Where the pencils hang on strings'. The dolly-tub full of lobby, that cheap but nourishing 'potbank stew' on which whole families used to be reared, has been replaced by the sterile plastic detritus of 'Food Trays'.

As might be expected, this world is haunted by ghosts – of drunken uncles, malcontent caretakers, boozers, the poet's father and the very soul of 'The Vanished Pit Village'. In 'A Fly in the Ointment' the revenant is all too corporeal: filthy and reeking of urine, 'the bearded' one returns daily to sit in the splendid new library to the disgust of its fastidious custodians. Even the dandelions are figured as spectres, 'ghosts of these rag suns blown away'. The poet is desperately cataloguing a disappearing world, each poem 'A Snapshot' of '[a] moment before it died forever'.

The birth of the artist as observer is recorded in 'Rustic Memory' – in a field, long ago, 'it was the first time/ I realised the sun was yellow'. The language of this poem mimics the simple syntax of the child's speech and in this follows James Joyce's technique in the opening of his 1916 novel *Portrait of the Artist as a Young Man*. In his own narrative of artistic development Arthur writes 'My pictures are all painted from my memory of the world I was reared in. Not so much the memory of any particular place or person, but more perhaps an essence of them.' His early established practice of painting from memory, rather than directly from life as advocated by the art school, also seems germane to the poetic task of distilling experience. The artist's struggle with the media and technique with which to render that essence is treated comically in 'How to Paint a Picture of Nile Street', where the speaker recommends such unconventional materials as pig's blood, cinders and soot. Arthur himself preferred the codge of mixed media on board. He had little patience with the careful techniques and meticulous draftsmanship that art schools attempted to teach and notes in the poem: 'In painting pictures, accidents of this kind/ Can often be fortuitous.' Thus it was that the world of codge formed the artist.

Arthur achieved in his painting a happy marriage of the modernist European tradition with local primitivism, most notably that of C.W. Brown of Biddulph Moor. The same can be said of the poetry, up to a point, though understandably his technique in this form did not develop to the same extent. Poetic tradition was dominated by formal rhyme scheme and metre until the early twentieth century when it was superseded, at least for the avant-garde, by so-called free verse. As dictated by Eliot, this did not legitimise poetic free-for-all but required even tighter precision and control of the part of the poet. Arthur's irregular rhyming and scansion sometimes appear to lack precisely such tight orchestration. He was more than aware of his own limitations as a poet but a snippet in the memoir is telling.

Arthur considers a pub song sung by a drunken Irishman with 'no idea of singing': '[h]e somehow turned its simple sentiments into something much richer until it became a song of perished black morter [sic] and perished bricks.' This magical transubstantiation of the medium is an ideal for Arthur, whatever the art form, along with an intimately close empathy with the subject. His poetic voice developed not in spite, but in part because of any perceived limitations. This voice has the capacity to draw the reader (even one from another time and place) into a rich and earthy world of pub singers and 'perished black morter'.

Talking of mistakes, the editor of this volume has had a pretty difficult job. The original typescript of *Dandelions* contains many errors of spelling and punctuation – chief among these being the misuse or omission of the now embattled possessive apostrophe. Even obvious errors were in the main reproduced by the typesetter in the 1993 edition. But since Arthur was both linguistically inventive and used some dialect words in his verse, it is sometimes difficult to decide on authorial intention. Some mistakes, if such they be, are fortuitous indeed. One example is the 'Miscagnegated' louts of 'Night'. The version in *On the Street* has the conventional 'Miscegenated', but 'Miscagnegated' is poetically apt as a harder sound suggesting some indeterminate and sinister maladaption peculiar to modern youth.

Another curious word is 'busky' of 'The Swilling Woman', corrected from 'busty' in the typescript. Its archaic meaning of bushy or shrub-covered might identify the Swilling Woman with a rural as well as domestic setting. It enhances her characterisation as a force of nature. We may also turn to the nation's iconic poet and playwright for further resonance. 'Busky' is used by Shakespeare in Act 5 of *Henry IV, Part I*: 'How bloodily the sun begins to peer/ Above yon busky hill.' However, the 1598 Quarto has 'How bloudily the sunne begins to peare/ Aboue yon bulky hill.' So it is that Shakespeare, who was himself writing before the modern standardisation of spelling and punctuation, bequeaths additional substance (were any such needed) to the busky/busty/bulky Swilling Woman.

It is of no little importance that Arthur makes us laugh; melancholy is leavened by 'bits of daft, thank goodness'. Like all the best eulogists, the poet embraces the comic quirks that characterised the dear departed. The simple pleasures of life – food and sex – are also celebrated, sometimes together. North Staffordshire's signature dishes are honoured with an Ode and Homage to Lobby and the Oatcake respectively. Women do not fare quite so well.

In triad 'A Watchman's Tale, 'Poem' and 'Our Mavis', the first exemplar of the fair sex is so voraciously greedy she has eaten her husband's pet rabbits. 'Our Mavis' is reputedly a 'trollopse' (another lovely word) and 'Poem' spells it out: young working-class women may be slim and beautiful, but chips and childbirth mean they soon run to fat.

The Bard of Burslem takes it upon himself to modernise Shakespeare's Sonnet 130: 'My mistress' eyes are nothing like the sun', subverting both the courtly love and carpe diem conventions in 'Pleasure Meter'. Here the speaker considers the physical charms of his lady love against such fleshly delights as pigs head brawn, beef dripping and pork pies (these dainties being themselves of lardy composition and mottled hue). Where Shakespeare mitigates insult with a decisive final couplet: 'And yet, by heaven, I think my love as rare/ As many she may belie in false compare', our poet remains undecided: 'but I can't really be sure/ which I like the best.'

In the three poems following: 'A Lost Love', 'Advice to a Young Man' and 'Prattle', women are presented as sexually rapacious, scorping harpies, whining, trivial and petty. Like the beef dripping foresworn in the memoir for the sake of the author's heart, working-class women have their obvious (if short-lived) charms but are fundamentally dangerous to the male of the species. Such poems suggest a somewhat unreconstructed consciousness. Suffice it to say, while the poetic speaker cannot simply be identified with the author, Arthur was probably more preoccupied with the decline of working-class culture than he was with emerging second-wave feminism. Smashing the patriarchy was neither here nor there when considering the demolition of an entire way of life.

Not unsurprisingly, the tame pastoral is an alien mode: Arthur stated not infrequently his distaste for nature, particularly as a child, and had apparently a liking for 'Artificial Flowers'. According to the memoir, his agoraphobia was born in the Moorlands. This country was, however, 'a tribal thing for me' and is rendered with bleak vigour in the paintings. Its landscape features in 'Bus Window', 'Hill Farm' and elsewhere in the second part, as do the people shaped by their harsh environment. It is likewise stalked by death and troubled by revenants in 'Winter', 'Enoch Adshead' and 'Lament for the Lump of Coal'.

While town and country meet in North Staffordshire, suburbia does not seem the author's natural habitat, an ill fit with his well-cultivated image. In the memoir, he writes dismissively of a local exhibition at the City Museum: 'the content was so genteel it was avenue painting for avenue walls, and they were avenue people who bought it.' Nevertheless, Arthur lived for years in Wolstanton, a suburb of the relatively genteel (compared with the adjacent Potteries) Newcastle-under-Lyme. He mentions in his introduction this 'later avenue life' and the 'privet hedges' which epitomise suburbia. There is gentle mockery in 'A Comfortable Old Age' and the 'neat and temperate garden' prissily shocked by riotous floral outburst in 'The Blossom'. But Larkinland is not our poet's spiritual home, so it is that the urban Potteries and bleak Moorland landscape dominate. The original collection ends where it began, with the faceless cruelty of modernity in 'The New Regime'; the impotence and infirmity of the ageing poet in 'The Telephone Message' and 'Sad Office Thoughts'.

This edition of *Dandelions* introduces four new poems: 'Town Hall in January' is a familiar Burslem scene; 'The Good Son' is a character companion piece, and 'What I Paint' follows 'Rustic Memory' along with 'How to Paint'. That Arthur dictated a poem in his final days strongly suggests the importance of poetry in his life. Death and infirmity have never been far away, but the last poem is at first glance quite incongruous. The bed of nails is a conventional metaphor for the suffering of the speaker. The original holy men associated with these devices were sometimes identified as fakirs, homophonous with 'fakers', suggesting the imposter syndrome felt by Arthur. Nails also summon the 'Man of Nazareth' of 'Easter Poem', as well as the romantic narrative of the artist as martyr. But in this poem, the defeat and disappointment that Arthur felt keenly at times in his life, signalled by Staffordshire's cricketing loss off stage, are sublimated to 'ecstasy', underscoring its religious element. What is even more surprising is the Home Counties reference with a traditionally upper-class sport to boot – prime Betjeman territory. But, as the poem contains covert reference to Arthur's home turf, its last words – 'my heart' – seal a cryptic love letter to the poet's place of origin.

Arthur Berry remains for my money Stoke-on-Trent's foremost poet by virtue of his ability to convey a vivid picture of a place and its people in a distinctive and hugely compelling voice. He, more than any other, is still the genius loci of this struggling post-industrial city. The common dandelion, the urban flower he claimed as his own, should also be that of the city, whose current inelegant motto could then be replaced with the more succinct Sicut Taraxacum – like the dandelion. This, of course, is fanciful, but it is happy fact that the perennial Potteries laureate is broadcast once again in this centenary year.

Catherine Burgass, 2025.

Dr Catherine Burgass is a retired university lecturer. She is currently writing a literary history of Stoke-on-Trent.

Editorial note

Dandelions exists in its original typescript with hand-corrections and in several printed editions. Some poems survive in annotated handwritten manuscript, and there are also audio and film recordings of Arthur Berry reading some of the poems aloud. Editorial details vary across these versions. This centenary edition reverts to the authority of the typescript in the first instance, and incorporates amendments of the first edition (1993) that appear to be intentional, as far as this editor can work out. The consistent inconsistency of the poet's work has thus been reproduced here as faithfully as possible.

In This Place

In this place
There are many compartments of
Compassion, Advice bureaux,
Many clinics and infirmaries
No one can fall through
Mind you there are long
Waiting lists
For treatment, many applications
For the remaining places
But it is quite impossible
Outside the proper channels,
There is much deliberation
Over the precise meaning
Of some particular word
It is most necessary
To find the proper category
And yet, in this place
Old allegiances are suddenly worn away
And even that which a man might think
He had saved, the proper accumulation
Of his days quickly disappears
And should he return
To the streets of his birth
He will find them recently demolished
By some remote decision
Some humane system of rehabilitation
Will no doubt have been found

In this place the streams are silted up
Or tunnelled to some
Sensible purpose
And covered by
A neat geometric bridge
In these days
After the early morning
The light becomes
As hard as steel.

The Trembling Motion

Sometime before
It was long before
I had ever noticed
Any trembling at the still centre
It was before I had worn my teeth away
When they still sliced green apples to the core
Before I knew who the dead were
When the muzzles of young dogs
Damp from their digging
Were wet in my hand
And the snows of those winters were higher than the
        beck of my cap
When whatever it was was only what it was
There was no trembling then
That was when the house was solid
Before the guttering was rotten with earwigs
Before the dry lice had turned the wood to powder.
Before the mind had become invaded
By the possibility of different identities
No, I cannot remember any trembling then.
But then, as quick or as slow as the grass grows
As winter comes or the snow goes
It was there. Shy at first
Hardly felt
Like the blood from a minor wound
Finding its way out
Into the outside world

Where it soon spread out
And the idiot mind would not leave it alone
But sought it out
With malevolence
As this was to become its bone
This constant trembling
At the centre of my world.

Here

How dense the light is here,
It sticks to the eyes
Like a blanket melted into a grey milk
Filled with fine plaster and spiders' legs,
As though the fine ash from some old explosion
Had never quite settled again.
Eyes that have been reared on a light like this
Will find it difficult to adjust to any other.
How rich the shadows are here.
As dark as the blackness out of old pits,
Or stoves. Or as deep as the dark
Of closed-in rooms. As black
As funeral hats, touched by the fumbling blind,
That have the feel of velvet, and lie
Forgotten in the bottoms of old wardrobes.
How delicate the colour of the earth is here,
An endlessly changing
Blue-purple of insects' wings
Turning into rust.

The Bulldozers

Will nothing slake the thirst of these monsters?
Maul and whine,
Smash and drag out,
They are covered with the dry scars of earth
Their bright yellow hides
Gleam through the fine plaster dust
Only the rare blood of old soldiers
Who are still fading away
In some pocket of other times
Still left in the side streets
Can assuage the thirst
Of these creatures.
My father's belt swings uneasily
On its nail on the back door.
My uncle's thin wrist shakes
As he holds his glass.
No place for the window cleaner with wild eyes
And a mania for gambling.
No place for the fat man
With a dirty shirt, who sells
Warm oat cakes
In the smoke room of public houses.
These are they whom the machines want.
The prefabricated buildings
Crumble sideways.
So lay your soft cheek
Against these bits of broken brick

Against these cinder scars,
The cool dockweed
The old cars
The empty kiln's open womb
The sleeping figure in the small back room,
The gable ends
Are breaking down
And the breath is going from this town
And another empire will soon be gone.

Wasteground

An acrid wind blows
Through this wilderness of bits,
This Golgotha of dead vehicles.
Their reared up bodies
Frozen stiff in their last agonies.
Here the trees have trunks of wet iron
And leaves of matted wire.
The grass is filled with iron spikes
And what flowers there are
Are withered in their sockets.
In the yellow water close by
A can floats through a skin of oil
Seeping out from the poisoned land.
All the birds here have clockwork voices
And beaks sharp as rusted razors.
All the men here have eyes
Filled with the venom of small steel rings,
The sun here is a bland eye of glass
That floats through clouds of sulphur gas.

Morning

Each morning
Along the beaten paths
By the shrouded water
Muffled up men
Come to the station
They buy their tickets
And sit in the waiting room
Smoking and coughing they greet each other
With some simple salutation
A coarse jest, or
Some sardonic remark
While they wait for the
Workmen's train to arrive
Through the window
Of the waiting room
The morning light is
As mysterious as a pearl
And above the houses
A pale phantom, this day's sun
Arises, over the near horizon
Of delicate chimneys, out of the mist
Of the still canal.

Orford Street

ORFORD STREET was condemned
All the houses were empty
The people had gone to
Another part of the city
All the doors and windows
Were boarded up
One house was buttressed
From the side
To stop it falling down
This house had no front door
And all its windows were
Smashed
In the front room of the house
The room that would
Have been called the parlour
All the floorboards had been
Ripped up
Split from their nails
As though by a madman in a frenzy
Possessed of great strength
Looking for something he had lost
The fireplace in this room
Was made of mottled tiles
Some of the tiles were broken
Some of them were missing
The firebasket was filled with ashes
And lying on the ashes

Was the dead body of a pigeon
With its withered claws
Clenched tight in its chest
As though in indignation
At what it had seen
In the corner of the room
There had been a gas meter
But it had been taken away
And the pipes hammered flat
Propped against these pipes
Was the remains of a fur toy of some kind
Holding its remaining limb
Awkwardly above its head
As though to ward off
Some intended blow
Above this sad toy
Suspended from the window of the room
Pinched and trapped
Was a garment of some kind
Hanging there, a limp suicidal thing
That had failed in its
Hysterical attempts to get away
From this hollow ruin

Ode to Lobby

Mother's Friend – A Potbank Stew

Mrs Florrie Baddeley
Of Leonora Street
Always swore by lobby
Her swore by other things as well
Syrup o' figs, goose oil,
As much Guinness as yer could get
But her swore by lobby
Most of all
Her always said it was only lobby
As erd pulled 'em through
When her'd been at her wit's end
To feed all her brood
And yer could understand it
As her'd had twenty-two
Her husband Alf had only
Got put his trousers on the
Bed and her was there again
He was a very lustful man
In drink. But Florrie always said
It was God's will
And in them days there was no
Such thing as the Pill
But when it was washing day
And all the children had come home from school
The house was like a hell hole
Full of squawking, blarting, hungry kids

So every other day Florrie would
Make a dolly tub full of lobby
And would ladle it out
And that erd shut ’em up
As they’d sit and spoon or suck it up
Her’d get a piece of scrag end or a lump er breast
For a copper or two
An onion, a carrot, and plenty er taters
And give ’em a round er bread ter dip in
And then they’d all go back school with a full belly
In the afternoon
While her pegged her washing out
The beauty of it was, Florrie said
Yer could put ’em lobby
Breakfast, dinner and tea
And they’d always clean it up
And the eldest lad
Was six foot two and only sixteen
Big enough ter be a bobby
And Florrie said it was because
He’d always been a
Good chucked ’un
And filled his belly every day with lobby
Talking of washing days
Mrs Ada Degg
Had a wooden leg
And on washing days
Would use it as a dolly peg

The Vanished Pit Village

Down by the canal and Ecclestone Street
Where the souls of dead colliers meet
Between the Salem chapel and the Lord Nelson Inn
A man on a racing cycle waits
By the level crossing gates
Waits for a line of shunted coal wagons to pass
Among wreaths of steam and smell of gas
Watched by a man, shaking a tin
To fetch his homing pigeons in
Fan tails and tipplers and youths playing cards
At the back of the old knackers yard
Down by the doors of the dole
Or some other God forsaken hole
Where old men cough in the betting shops
And huge fat women queue in the Co-op
And gangs of screaming kids
Banging on ash-bin lids
Run down the damp and sour streets
Between the lines of drying sheets
To get a place in the chip shop queue
Before it's time to go back to school
Six of chips and a jar of peas
And put salt and vinegar on, will you please
The aerial ropeways are delicate and clear
And so are the fan row the chain row and
The pit head gear.

The Chain Row, 1994

Dandelions

Where the end of the wall
And the waste ground meet
At the back of the canal
And Navigation street
Dandelions bold as brass
Grow among the bitter grass
In this place of empty chapels and aborted kilns
By the still smouldering fires
That burn the mattresses of the recently dead
These sour yellow flowers raise their heads
Damp rag suns that shine
On the sides of a lost loop line,
Among wild lupins and cinders
Fed on the dried excrement of dogs
Among the canal's wet clinging fogs
Hard flower suns that gleam
By the edges of the poisoned stream,
Where the hiss and slip
Of a rat nuzzles against the dead body of a cat
Among the slime and burning lime
And down in the flattened cemetery
Where my drunken uncles lie,
Over the iron gate
Into a bland white sky
Ghosts of these rag suns are blown away
Into the passing traffic of the day.

The Procession

When I was a boy
Every Sunday afternoon
With my clean jersey on, my fringe combed
And my shoes blacked
I joined a procession
Of big lads and little kids
To go a walk to the fields. Before long
The little kids were usually blarting
And wanting ter go home
So we always stopped at a Sunday shop
To buy liquorice torpedoes or bags of kali
To shut them up
And then we used to knock at a woman's door
Who sold herb beer
And ask her if she would
Fill our empty pop bottles with water
When we'd all had a suck at this
We went down the allotment paths
Passed the old men with fantails and tipplers
And watched the pigs in the pig sties
And the hens pecking among the cabbage stalks
Then we climbed a fence
And slid down the railway cutting
Among the foxgloves and the dandelions
And dug for pig nuts
And threw bricks in the canal
And then one week I caught scarlet fever
From a grid

My throat was covered in yellow spots
So they wrapped me in a red blanket
And took me in an ambulance
To the fever hospital
Where they stuck a shiny thing
Down my throat
And starved me for seven weeks
And when I came out
The procession had gone
And I could never catch
Them up again
I could hear 'em
And I have seen the little stiff tailed dog
Just turning a corner
But I could never catch 'em
I once saw 'em
At the jampot wakes
That comes here every year in August
Some stalls
And some dobby horses
I'm sure it was them
They were standing round
A little stall listening to a
Woman shouting
Her'd got a dirty-faced baby
And an Alsatian dog
As was blind in one eye
Since then I've never seen 'em again
But once I dreamed of 'em
And I could hear the little kids
Blarting wanting to go home

Three Uncles

I had an uncle called Sam
He used to tell me
The back of his head was stuck on with jam
And when I was a little kid
I used to believe it did
And I remember
I would sit and stare
At the back of his thinning hair
Hoping perhaps to see some jam
Oozing from my Uncle Sam
I had another uncle they called Jud
He could make all the tap rooms of this town laugh
As he played his hands of crib
Or on the snooker handicap
He spent a lot of his time
In the Salamanca Inn
His poor wife went to work to keep him
I remember he gave me a cap badge
Of the Royal Artillery
On which the wheel of the cannon
Went round and round.
When they laid poor Jud in the ground
Those who were at the funeral said
That he'd still play cards even though he was dead
That is, of course, if there was any a chance.
My third uncle was as thin as string
His knuckles were like the twisted roots
Of a holly tree. His long feet

Were misshapen with carbuncles
And he had no rubber in the peak of his cap.
In his workhouse bed
Just before he went dead
I watched his twisted fingers
Fumbling the silver wrapper
On a chocolate bar
And I heard him whistle
Oh, how he could whistle
He could whistle all the melodies of his lost days
All the love songs of his wasted heart.

Snapshot

It was taken on a bus trip to the sea
Before the war
Long before the war was ever thought of
Just look at their faces under their caps
Flushed with bottle beer
Over and back, down the track of time
Over the hump of the war
Back into the moment of those smiles
Some laughing triviality
Trapped in an instant of light
The figures smile back
Your Bert, our Jack
Walking along the promenade
Strange children with ice cream cones
In the background looking on.
The line of the distant sea glints in the sun
Municipal deck chairs stacked against
The promenade railings
Coloured pennants blowing in the wind.
All those who are now dead
Smiling there in their 50 shilling suits
All is lost somewhere in between
The celluloid and the sunshine
Of a lost summer,
A world is trapped
A moment before it died forever.

A Man in Boote Street

Among the idlers and the rag-bone men
Who live in this street of broken windows
There is an effeminate man
Who wears a ginger wig.
He is tall, very tall,
Taller than the windows,
Taller than the doors,
And as he wanders about
Muttering to himself all day
He pushes an old pram,
With a bird cage in it
With an artificial bird.
The bird's feathers are made
Of empty cigarette packets
And its beak has been cut
From a splintered bit of stick.
Its legs are fashioned from
Pieces of rusty barbed wire
Tied on with string.
Altogether it is a poor
And shabby thing,
But as he pushes it up and down
He speaks to it
And then he attends to its balance
He whistles at it
As though it might sometime
Whistle back.

They say round here
That when he was a baby
Sitting sucking his dummy
In his pram,
The Salvation Army band
Passing by
Opened up full blast
And blew what brains
He'd got to smithereens.

Homage to the Oatcake

Let us pay homage to the Oatcake
Or Ootcake or woodcake as the old men called them
The oatcake is not a cake at all really
Not like the fairy cake or the Eccles cake
Not a cake in that way
More of a Potteries Papadum
A sort of Tunstall Tortilla
A Clay Suzette
As flat and thin as a dishcloth
An obedient and suppliant cheek
That will bend any way you want it
Round and floppy, the Oatcake
Has a texture similar to the
Skins of old colliers or men
Dying of Potters Rot
These are not cakes made for every day
And should only be eaten twice
Or at the most three times a week
Preferably at weekends when you are flush
And filled with drink
Or the prospect of drink
Such richness every day would be too much
Rather like having the News of the World
Delivered as a morning paper
There would surely be a drop in production
And an explosion in the birth rate
NO! Oatcakes are best eaten at weekend

And all genuine Oatcake shops are shut in the week
And their proprietors lie late abed
And spend the rest of the day
Watching horse racing on the tele
I have heard it said that small fortunes
Are made in this trade
And among the Potteries working class
When a child is born
There can be no higher hope for it
Than it could become a
Proprietor of a damned good
Oatcake and Pikelet shop
The Pikelet you ask, what's that?
It's a sort of female Oatcake
Smaller, thicker, sweeter
More immediately seductive
Sometimes with currants in it
A muffin for the Lumpen working class
Best eaten soaked in butter or marge
If over indulged in
Both these cakes can play the very
Devil with your waistline
I must warn
Indulgence leads to Bulgence.

Lanky Fred

He always said "You're a long time dead"
Did lanky Fred
When he was alive, in his life
After he had buried his wife
And the air was thick
With summer dust and cobwebs
And the heavy bodied bees
Staggered from the dahlias
To the sweet peas
When the dog rose grew in
The hawthorn hedge
And there were
Wild foxgloves
At the back of the well
When the pig styes
In the next allotment
Began to smell
And thick stems of dandelions
Grew between the sunken bricks
Of his garden path
Lanky Fred would sit in his little shed
And spit outside on the path
His mouth black from chewing twist
His dry skinned hands had
Blue birds tattooed on the wrists
And his cord trousers were held up
By braces and a brass buckled belt

If Fred spoke honest
About what he felt
He'd never been better off in his life
Since he'd buried
His clean hard-working wife
And now he was free as you might say
To do as he pleased
And have his own way
To spend all his pension on twist and drink
And be damned to what
The neighbours think
When his poor wife was alive
They had to make ends meet
By selling tomatoes,
Rhubarb and mint
And Fred was very often skint
Him and his little stiff-tailed dog
Were often as dry
As a lime-burner's clog.

They Are Gone

They are gone
Percy Clegg, and Uncle Tom,
Where is the blind man and his dog
Him that cleared the drains out with his clog
Where is the drunken ex-Town Clerk
The little man who wouldn't work
Where is the wild-eyed window cleaner
Who lived rough
The old woman who took snuff
Where is the vast fat man
With a painted tie
Him that had a monocle in his eye.
I remember one night in the smoke room
He sold us a little glass swan
God knows where he got them from
I wonder what happened to Shanghai-Lil
You would have thought she would have been
Too tough to kill
Where are the Angel
The Black Swan
The pulled-down Star
They are gone
They are gone
Even such as these are gone.

Shanghai Lil, 1993

Concrete Blocks

There is a kind of concrete block that crumbles
much favoured by councils for building low walls
it is I suppose a cheap stand-in for stone
which it superficially resembles in texture and tone
but not in shape as each block is a rectangular cube
at least it is when it is first laid down
there must be thousands of these low, false stone walls
on council estates of the town
they were used to divide and subdivide
house from house and garden from pavement
a seemingly cheap and easy to handle means
of marking out boundaries of each council house
these blocks were made in moulds
filled with rough granules of compressed concrete
each mould exactly like the rest
I have known local entrepreneurs
to take disused chapels over
and manufacture these blocks
I cannot say they make fortunes out of it
but I can say they all appeared to be comfortably off
but then such men are quick to see opportunity
and the concrete block was simple to make
only rudimentary technology was necessary
to manufacture these imitation stones
and so these fake stone walls
two blocks high with a thinner
narrower concrete copingstone on top appeared.

At first they seemed a neat solution
to the demarcation problems
but soon after the first winter frosts
had got at them
and the gangs of bored children
had filched off the coping stones
the walls began to erode and crumble
and soon whatever geometry the blocks
had once possessed was gone
and they began to resemble
dumplings or pulpy grey concrete gums
rather than stone walls
and after a few years of this treatment
these raddled battlements
were hardly high enough for passing dogs to piddle on.

Food Trays

Each morning the streets
are littered with food trays
they lie among the leaves and fag packets
oblong, aching, white
under the morning sky
these food trays
are a shallow stand-in for a plate
a great convenience to chip shop proprietors
they will if held flat
contain the mush and slop
of gravy and wet peas
most of these plates are stained
with traces of these
but some are dead white
testifying to the gluttony of the people
who must have licked them clean last night
sometimes alas the diners eyes
have been bigger than their bellies
and they have overfaced themselves
and they have chucked the food they couldn't eat away
some of it of course stuck to the tray
nothing is more naked and dead
then the corpses of chips and peas
that have lain out all night
next morning they are a ghastly sight
these food trays will not rot
only split and flatten if trodden underfoot

they are a very ingenious invention
there must be thousands of them used each night
but for all their convenience
in the mornings they are a depressing sight
reminders of a weakness of will
and last night's lust
convenience troughs that turn a nose into a snout.

Polish Joe

By the main gate of the municipal park
There is a drinking fountain set in the wall
Where a rough iron cup is held by a chain
And the surrounding glazed bricks are shaped like a shell
Today I saw drinking there a tramp known hereabouts as
Polish Joe
Who carries all his worldly belongings in parcels hung
around his neck
It is said that he was a high-ranking officer
Some even say he was a General
Certainly, when he is not the worse for drink
He is filled with dignity
Whenever he lights one of the cigarette ends he finds in
the gutter
He carefully fixes it into an amber holder he carries and
Smokes it with a flourish
He also has a pair of trousers with a red stripe down the
legs
But as for being a General, well today there was no
mistaking he was one of the dregs
His unshaven Slavonic face was raw red, the blue-veined
nose almost black
And his gestures seemed to be theatrical and forced, and
his mouth was slack
Certainly, he did not resemble a man of breeding by any
stretch of the imagination
But perhaps no man could in his situation

Years of sleeping rough and drunkenness
Must have brutalized his features
And surely no ex-General would
Carry all his worldly belongings in parcels round his neck
And spend his days
Meandering through the streets of this city
Drunk on the dreadful Mojo
A cheap concoction of methylated spirits and either wine
or pop
Drink that would make an iron man drop
But to men like Polish Joe and their like
The stuff is as good as mother's milk
And sustains them through the drunken haze of their lives
He had been up in court a time or two
Mostly for drunkenness and urinating in grids
Much to the pleasure of the local kids
I believe he is entitled to a pension he never bothers to
collect
For something he did in the last war
But it was all such a long time ago
It must have stopped having any meaning for Polish Joe
Who's now become one of the dregs
Well known for smartly saluting folks as he begs.

Speaking of Fowl

Speaking of fowl
fowl in the way of feathered things that is
cock chickens, hens, pullets, poultry etc.
not foul in the way of drains or bad weather
or fowl is foul, not that sort of thing
but fowl in a feathered way,
today I was walking down dogmuck backs
behind Pynest Street
where I saw a Mrs Fowler plucking a
chicken in her back yard
As she plucked its feathers off
she felt the fresh plucked flesh
lovingly as though it may have been her own
She is a thin and horny woman
hr nose is like a beak
made of beak stuff stiff and shiny
her nostrils are long and sore and narrow
as though she may peck for her food
her hands and legs resemble claws
all her veins have dried twisted and knotted
in a peculiar way hard and lumpy
her throat's like the throat of a cock chicken
a ridged and wrinkled spout
forever jerking up and down
causing the ridges to telescope in and out
Her husband Len has a bump on his head
like an egg

he spends a good deal of his time on the lavatory
Seeing them both together it is is difficult
to imagine they have ever been
Young and supple enough
to engage in the act of copulation human style
but they must have managed it some time
because they have produced daughter called Sandra
who works behind the cooked meats counter at the Co-op
She's round and blonde and featureless
as though she may not have been born
but hatched from an egg with a very soft shell
that is, except for her hair
which is the colour of translucent bacon fat
The Fowlers are an affectionate family
Mr Fowler particularly is a very loving man
who calls his wife chick
and his daughter duck
but like all families they have their ups and downs
and when the women get
bloody-minded, ill-tempered and fed up
Mr Fowler keeps them both in check
by giving them a peck
on the back of the neck

The Wallpaperer

I once knew a man who papered rooms
all kinds of rooms he papered
and staircases too
he would paper anything this paperer would
he would have papered the sky
if he could have got a pair of steps tall enough
wherever he went
he always carried with him
a bucket and a flat brush
a portable wallpapering box
and a book filled with paper samples
the book must have been nearly a foot thick
inside it was every kind of wallpaper
the mind could possibly imagine
papers with flower patterns, papers covered with red roses
severe papers with simple stripes
and papers covered in delicate posies
embossed papers, criss crossed papers
and papers so richly covered in velvet
they would have done credit
to the walls of Buckingham Palace
the wallpaperer's book of samples had them all
all the walls in the streets round here
had been smoothed by his flat hands
when he was in the neighbourhood they
would shiver in expectation
when he died, they put his book of samples

in his coffin with him
and papered the insides of it with
a paper heavily embossed with gold

The Forgotten Sicilian

Bit by bit
Chip by chip
Night by night
The image of the previous proprietor
Is gradually eroded.
He was a Sicilian.
A thick necked
Fuzz haired man
Much plagued by boils.
His wife was a gentle
Nervous creature
Who tried her best,
But the effort of
Rearing a big family
And serving in a chip shop
Till after midnight each night
Was too much for her,
And her nose and eyes
Became bigger and bigger
And her smile needed constant
Propping up.
So it was as well,
They should return
To the island of
Sun and sulphur.
The present proprietor
Is also a Sicilian.

A very different one however.
He has the hawk nose
Of many of his people
And his forearms are
Covered with black hairs.
He is a very smiling gold-toothed man
Affable to everybody
And talks a great deal,
Although he hardly knows the language
Already he has introduced
A number of changes, and innovations.
For instance
He sells cheap imitation gold fountain pens.
These cost only ten pence each
But have a very expensive look about them.
A solicitor or a doctor could have one
Peeping from the top of his waistcoat pocket
And no one would ever guess
That he had given only ten pence for it.
These pens sell like wildfire,
And so do the pork sausages
The second innovation.
These pale sausages
Are dipped into
The hot sizzling fat
And in a few seconds
They come out golden brown,
And when these beauties
Are married to the chip
They torpedo very quickly

Any resolution I might have made
To avoid this chip shop
In consequence of my
Rapidly expanding waistline.

Broken Reverie

Sitting in a local café
having a round of toast
and a mug of sweet tea
I was reading about
the shattered third marriage
of a now fallen film star
when the door opened
and two young women with pushchairs entered.
"Two teas and two bacon sandwiches and a glass of milk,
    duck, please," one shouted, sitting herself down
at a formica topped table
and at once lighting a fag.
Her baby, a fat, dirty-faced child,
began to scream.
The other woman, a chinless creature
with slack stockings
pulled her pushchair between the tables
and tried to pacify the screaming child
with no success.
Her own child
a baby with a big head
and a chalk-white face
who didn't look as though
it was for this world long,
sat sucking a pink dummy tit.
This child stared at me
with unblinking eyes

and then opened its mouth
and without warning was sick.
I turned my head away
and tried to read the gossip column
about the doings of the rich,
but it was no use.
The fallen star seemed
suddenly very far away.
So I finished my toast
and drank my tea
and wished the patiently smiling proprietor
Good Day.

The Watchman's Tale

As the rain played on the tin roof
Of the workman's cabin
Various voluptuous young females
Smiled down from coloured photographs
Pinned to the wall
The old watchman paid no attention to them
As he poked the hard clinker
In the stove pot
With the handle of a broken spade.
"I used to keep rabbits," he said'
"But my missus used to eat 'em all
'Er must be seventeen stone if er's an ounce
Why, man, her'd eat a man
Off his horse and think nothing of it
All 'er ever thinks of is 'er belly
She would eat a raw monkey, if
There was any chance."
He drew a cigarette out of his tin
And drawing the smoke deep into his lungs
Said wistfully, "When I married her, her was only
A bit of a slip of a wench
No thicker then than a strip lath
You'd never think it to see her now though."

Poem

Working class women
Are often very fat
You've only to sit against them
On a bus,
To be aware of that,
Having lots of children
And always eating chips
Has caused them to burst out sideways
From their ever stretching zips
Their daughters though
Are often very beautiful creatures
Young and slim
With finely balanced features
Their hair is frizzed
Proud as Hadendoah's
Their eyes are dark
And arrogant as an expensive whore's
They view the world
Very differently
From their poor fat mothers.

Our Mavis

The drunken trollopse
Her mother said
Up and down the pubs of this town with that bloke Stan
Him as earns his living as a rag and bone man
All her thinks about is getting herself dolled up
Her never as much as washes a cup
And her wears her skirt up round her arse
I've told her again and again
What happens to wenches as court ragbone men on carts
Who spend all their lives in chip shops and pubs
Why, her never gets in the house till after twelve at night
And then her's a bloody sight
One night he'd knocked her black and blue
Her knows what to expect if her gets in the club
Her father will call her a bloody whore
And show her the wrong end of the front door
And then God only knows whatever her will do
I know I'm at my wit's end
Trying to make her see sense
But I might as well talk to that cat
For all the notice she takes
And I know her'd take no notice of me
If I talked myself blue in the face
All her does is stand in front of the mirror
Painting her face
And flaunces herself about
Without a care in her head

Her says her's only young once
And her's going to enjoy herself while her can
Having a good time with that bloke ragbone Stan
Her can't see to him her's no more than a bit of skirt
And when he's had what he wants he treats her like dirt.

Welfare State Blues

Roses round the door
Babies on the floor
Who could wish for more
Than sleepy valley
Down below the dole line
Where the bottom quarter live
The big day is Friday, pay day
The day of Resurrection
You can say that again, kid
The once a week ship comes in day
The supplementary pension day
The day of the butter voucher
Never mind what they say.
Down by the skint-by-Tuesday brigade
You can forget Sunday
It's God send Friday all the way
Down the corridors of the powerless
Where the pencils hang on strings
In the cubicles of the offices of the social
Harassed clerks in cardigans
Dispense whatever the proper entitlements
God bless this house
Never a truer word spoken
Under the posters warning of Blackfly, Greenfly
Foul pest, potato blight, swine vesicular disease,
Gonorrhoea, diarrhoea, VD and the rest
The wives of unemployed window cleaners

Threadbare dandies, part-time tattooists,
Ex-bin men with double ruptures
Alcoholic chefs, addleheads, pinheads,
Honest clerks and loud-mouthed shitheads
With hanging trouser arses, flyboys
And water headed idiots led by their mothers
And reasonable men, genuine victims
With polished shoes, hoping and hoping
All ring the bell for attention
While in the doctors' surgeries among
The prams and blarting babies smelling of
Dried piss and napkins, uncles and aunties
And big girls in see-through
Panties, every third one up the spout,
Wait for their prescriptions
Nervous breakdowns, shingles, varicose veins,
Or depression, see the psychiatrist for a
Session, Vallium, Librium,
Electric shock, the Pill or abortion
Then back on your back again
What a caution
Her hair was like a burst old sofa
Her eyes were like supperating ulcers
The day they took her
Now she's better
All nine kids in institutions
So she sits quiet all day on the sofa
Like a zombie
Living on crisps and pop and Mars bars
Staring for hours and hours through the window

As the forever and ever women pass
Pushing their endless pushchairs
Their great bloomered chip-reared
Haunches squashing their bootees flat,
Down below the dole line
Far beyond the last demand for payment
Where the licence dodgers
Lie in bed all day
In the never never land
Among the old saloons and bangers
Adenoidal children scream
For plain or cheese and onion
And among the hopheads and the nutters and
Old men spitting in the gutters
I can hear the phlegm-filled voices singing
Rule Britannia and Lester Piggott
Hallelujah
God Save the Queen and Missus Thatcher
And roll on Friday for God's sake, roll on Friday
The day thou givest Lord is ended
Till next Friday
Keep dipping your bread in, kid
Roses round the door
Babies on the floor
Who could wish for more
Than sleepy valley

The Ex Bus Cleaner

The retired bus cleaner is sad
His son-in-law is not to his liking
Nor does his unmarried daughter please him
It seems that this string-thin creature
Sits by the fire all day wiping her nose
And looking through the mail order catalogues
At the women's clothes
But certainly the biggest cross he has to bear
Is his complaining wife
Who works part-time washing up in a café
She has whined his faults at him
Every day of their married life
His biggest fault according to her
Is his liking for drink
In his younger days he was a well set up youth
Quite a dandy up and down the town
All the latest styles in haircuts and dress
A good footballer too by all accounts
That was until he hurt his knee
It was then he met his missus at a dance in the Town Hall
And he took her home and pressed her up against the wall
Next thing yer know he'd got her up the stick
And that was that
He often reminisces now about when he was a lad
And speaks of his father
Who liked a finger of cheese

And a half pint of draught beer
Every night before he went to bed
The old man's been forty years dead
He died on Boxing Day
After watching Blackburn Rovers play Stoke
Blackburn won four one
It must have upset him that much
As when he got back home he dropped dead
He was a big Stoke supporter in his day
He'd walk through rain and snow fer watch 'em play
Beer was tuppence a pint then
Yer could get drunk and have a packet er fags for a bob
But then my missus 'as always been
Bigoted against drink
But damn and blast her I say
If I couldn't get my four pints a night
I should never sleep a wink
I should be twisting and turning restless in bed
To tell yer the truth if I couldner have a drink
I might as well be
Six foot under the clod

Night Noises

Lying watching the shadow
of the window blind
listening to nothing
waiting for sleep
I heard footsteps
down in the street
footsteps that began to run
and then stopped
or were stopped
then a stifled cry
a slight muffled scream
that stopped
or was stopped
all my attention
suddenly focussed
trying to read
the noise
it was probably
the next door neighbour's
hell cat son
who often bashes girls about
but still they come
there, there's the noise again
not a stifled cry or a scream
but a word, no! no!
and then the voice stopped
or was stopped

I listened and
could hear no more
then hid and turned my head
hopefully to sleep
when I heard a young girl's voice
clear and bitter
she spat the words out
you swine
you swine
she said it twice
and the silence and the darkness
framed the sound
and I listened and listened
but there was no noise
nothing else
for a few seconds or maybe more
and then I heard
the next door's
front door
pulled to with a slam
next day as I passed
down the entry which divides
our house and next door
I saw a small rolled up ball
it was a pink handkerchief
damp and small
lying against the edge
of the pavement
and the entry wall

Girl at Night

A soft blonde girl
With thick ankles
Her hair all dishevelled
Came running out of the darkness
Of a side street
On to the lighted pavements
Of the main road
She stood for a moment
Sheltering in the doorway
Of a furniture shop
As she caught sight of herself
In the reflection from the window
She began to straighten her hair
And do a quick repair
To her flustered face
Then she looked up
At the town hall clock
Glanced up and down the street
Had a good look at her feet
Decided which direction she wanted to go
And disappeared into the darkness.

Suicide

In the back bedroom
of sixty seven Amicable Street
a man is lying flat on his back
on a single bed
He is dead
there is silver spittle on his lips
nobody knows he's dead yet
the objects in the room do not know
that he is not just asleep
he bed he lies on is unaware
on a small table
at the side of the bed
is a bottle of tablets
some of the tablets have fallen on the floor
lying on the bed at the side of the man
is a prayer book open at the twenty-third Psalm
The Lord is my Shepherd, I shall not want
He maketh me to lie down in green pastures
He restoreth my soul.
The bedspread the man is lying on is green
the room is neat
the man had pulled his shoes off
before he got on the bed
his jacket hangs on a hanger
on the back of the bedroom door
the only things out of place are the tablets
fallen on the floor

on the other side of the bed
there is a red leatherette stool
with polished steel legs
on this stool there is a packet of paper handkerchiefs
above the bed there is a chandelier
a cheap glass chandelier
such as may be bought from
most department stores
out in the world
outside the bedroom
down in the backs
sitting on the backyard wall
is the man's cat
it sits there oblivious of his death
the cat occasionally licks its paws
it is a striped cat
dappled in a strange way
it has a yellow collar with a bell
round its neck
and as it sits it stares up at
a celluloid windmill
fixed to the top of a pole
although there is no wind
the windmill goes round and round
and as it does it makes a little whistling sound

Artificial Flowers

In the bedroom window
Of number forty four
There are three artificial flowers
In a pot.
They are imitation hyacinths
Arranged a little stiffly
Like the fingers of an outstretched hand.
They are very realistic
Excellent imitations of the real thing
In fact you would be hard put to,
To tell the difference.
The white bowl they stand in however,
Is very harsh in its shape
You can tell it is plastic
By the way it shines
But all in all
The total effect is very satisfactory.
Considering the street, the house,
The way the curtains fall,
The colour of the bricks
And the pebble dash
It is all quite satisfactory.
Perhaps even more
In a way, rather splendid,
Each piece seems to fall
Together like a jigsaw puzzle
And makes a kind of

Accidental perfection
Of the bedroom window of forty four
Goodfellow Street.

How to Paint a Picture of Nile Street

To paint a picture of Nile Street
One would need a warped plywood board
Some glue, a sack bag, some rusty screws,
A basinful of pig's blood, a small bag of soot,
Some crushed cinders, a scrubbing brush,
Moonlight, bakelite, spit, a piece of stick, a pin,
A comb for special effects, and a wet sponge.
Having got all these things
The first thing to do
Is to screw the warped board down
Flat with the rusty screws,
And then cover it carefully with the sack bag
And glue it down.
If the bag lies unevenly, do not despair
It is all perhaps for the best.
In painting pictures, accidents of this kind
Can often be fortuitous.
Now mix the pig's blood with the soot
For the colour of bricks,
And use the crushed cinders for the mortar.
Crushed cinders have been found very suitable for this.
Then get the scrubbing brush
And scrub the colours in, scrub the paint on
Then scrub it off again, until the sack bag
Is nearly rubbed off the plywood base,
Then leave it to dry,
But before it is dried completely

Get a piece of chalk, and either
Write the name of someone you love
Or, better still, draw the body of a naked woman
On the bricks. This may be difficult, but do your best,
Then from somewhere collect some tin bottle tops
And melt them to make a wash of moonlight
To cover the sky and gutters with.
Now get the dry stick
And carefully begin to draw
All the windows and the doors
Until you get to number twenty three,
Then don't forget, whatever else you do
To draw the cobbler who works in the front room,
He has a nose that sweats
And a canary with one leg.
Try to contrive to give him plenty of light
The nails he uses are so small
And his eyes are not what they were.
I'll tell you what, draw a lamp post outside his door
It would help light his parlour on winter afternoons
It would also be useful for the dogs in the street
To sniff and piddle on as they pass.
Now try to make a mixture to paint the windows,
This may be elusive, and I am afraid
There is no formula, it is much to do
With the quality of changing light.
But if you get a pin and draw spiders webs
In the corner of each window it often helps
To create an elusion of glass,

Something to hang your hat on, so to speak.
Now the painting should be done,
And I should turn its face to the wall
For a few hours, or even a full day.
Then I should turn it back and get a sponge
Of wet turpentine and wipe it all away,
And if people should ask you why
You destroyed it, tell them
It was only painted for a day.

Hoppo

Albert Hopwell,
The lodging house keeper is dead.
I heard the news from one of his lodgers,
In the Public Reading room.
He will be sadly missed.
Hoppo, as he was called, was an important man
In the half-world in which he lived.
He was a master of claims and benefits,
A poor man's lawyer in fact.
His advice was always free for the asking
Often given as he sat all through the winter nights
Clasping and unclasping his transparent thin-nailed hands
In front of the gas fire in the tap room
Relishing the drink and the heat,
He has set many a poverty-stricken illiterate
On the way to claiming his rights.
He, himself drew compensation and bought
The lodging house with the money.
His lungs were eaten away with pit dust
And often when he was swilling his lodging house out
With a bucket of disinfectant and a mop
He used to damn near cough his lungs
Up in the bucket.
But for all that his breathing was so bad,
He always had a wet fag end
Hanging from the skin of his bottom lip.
His cap and coat

Were the colour of old floorcloths
And his eyes were blood-veined misty yellow yolks,
Yet his glance was sharp and his talk filled with wit
He was an expert at the snapping up of small bets
The names of champions were regularly on his lips,
Philadelphia Jack O'Brien, Jack Sharkey,
Two Ton Tony, and the Panama Kid
And not only the fighters' names were known to him
But the place and attendance at their fights.
He had a photographic memory it was said
He used to study the Guinness Book of Records
till late in the night
Now such a man is gone who will mourn him?
He will be mourned by men who have put their hopes on
 horses
Men that have lived beyond their women
And those who were always too ill-shaped to love,
And so loved drink.
Men that have eaten the bitter bread
And have stared at the rough salt-cellar when
There has been nothing else to see,
And laughing men, who have boozed their dead wives'
 club money
And those that sleep late and stand waiting
For opening time
These will mourn him in their own fashion.
There will be no scattering of ashes that is for sure.
A word, a nod, a cough as the blue fag smoke rises
Like a wreath in the tap room window

For these men who sit by the gas fire in The Dolphin
Are not men of ceremony
It is sufficient to
Remember and be there
That is all.

A Night Out With Tut

I went out with Tut the other night
And we had a lot of laughs,
A lot of little laughs.
All night long we were bursting into laughs,
Everything he said made me laugh
Just anything at all.
Maybe he'd said it had been
A nice day
And there we were
Laughing again.
All little laughs,
Giggle laughs,
No real belly laughs,
Just daft laughs,
All about nothing.
Hysterical laughs
And him as bad as me.
I only had to catch his eye
And we were at it again,
I'd laugh at him, and he'd
Laugh at me,
Anybody watching us
Must have thought we were round the bend.
I could have understood it
If we'd have been pissed
But we'd only had a couple of pints
Of mild and bitter

And then we started this tittering
And it just wouldn't stop
I tried to pull myself together
Before the night became a delirium
But it was no use.
I'd catch a glimpse of him,
Maybe lighting a fag
Or just putting one out,
And for some reason it would strike me as funny
And I would start sniggering
And then he'd join in.
It got to such a pitch
We had to leave the Pub
And go out in the night air
Where it was cooler.
That stopped us laughing at last
And Tut said he felt sick.
Not sick in his stomach
But sick in his head
And a feeling of nausea
Had come over me too
And suddenly I felt really rotten.
As we said goodnight
And I took a breath
Of the night air
I was suddenly overcome
By a sagging sense of despair.

The Bus Shelter

It is after closing time
And the usual people are there in the bus shelter
Waiting for the bus
The bus shelter is a construction
Of metal and glass
With four long panes down each side
With an opening to go in
And an opening to go out
On one of the solid ends
It has an image of a huge glass
Filled with stout
With a splendid froth on the top
Advertising the pleasure
Of drinking at home
In the shelter
There is a shrivelled
Up old dandy
Wearing a cheap mohair coat
I noticed that he has
Silver buckles on his shoes
He's evidently been out
Looking for a bit of life
On his third finger he wears
A large signet ring
I should not think it was of great value
But among the company who frequent
The bar of the local hotel

It gives him the air of opulence
Behind him in the queue is a man
With a bald head with a
Lump on the top of it
Some cyst or other no doubt
His wife carries a white poodle
With an aquamarine studded collar
The dog stares over her shoulder
Blinking its intense little eyes
At a man with a pipe-sucking ferret's face
Who has a British Legion badge
Pinned to the lapel of his
Port wine coloured blazer
The man standing behind him
Has lips like crushed worms
And burning hot ears
And I cannot understand
However he came to choose
As the woman to share his bed
The creature who holds on
To his arm
She is a thin bone of a woman
With a white powdered skin
Her legs are no thicker than a hen's
And seem to be made of the same stuff
She is always whining and her nose is
Slightly sore at the end
Oh yes and then there is the cheery cripple
Don't let's forget him

He's well known to them all
His crippledom has become a role
He plays for all he's worth
Never a dull moment
There's a spirit for you
With him it's pal this and pal that
Let's all be pals
And then standing directly
In front of me
There is a woman I have often desired
Her head seems to exist in a halo of space
I wonder how she would be
Lying naked in bed
She has a coarse sensual face
And a calculating hard lipped mouth
Her husband left her long ago
And since she has taken many uncles back
To her three children
The one she has tonight has thin well-brushed hair
And a luminous blue raincoat
And for some reason he keeps consulting
His wristwatch
Then he whispers something in her ear
And she laughs a promising laugh
And as I watch her black hair
And the shining earring
Fixed to the soft lobe of her ear
I envy him the pleasure he has to come

Drinking Men

Drinking men
Often die lonely deaths
These who have forsaken women
And have died in their camaraderie of booze.
When it comes to their time
And they lie prostrate and helpless
In a ward in some public institution,
They can expect few visitors,
Except for those who cannot for shame
To keep away
And sit with them reluctantly
Some soft hearted daughter or niece perhaps,
Let us hope that these
Have the grace
To keep any admonishment to themselves
And draw what comfort they may have
From the thought
Of their dutiful husbands.
Men who have faced
Up to their responsibilities
And not drunk
Every penny they could get their hands on.

No Change

I have heard it said
That every dog has its day
But some of the dogs round here
Have not had theirs yet,
Mind you they still have a bet
And hope for something to turn up
And of course they have had seasons
That were better
And seasons that were worse
But mostly their efforts
End up in a stifled curse
I suppose things round here
Have always been much the same
Time repeating the old games again
There's certainly been no great
Beauty born. Things if anything
Seem a little more worn
That's all, barring the occasional
Sudden collapse or
An excruciating pain
Soon forgotten under the rain
Of comings in and goings out
Certainly nothing to shout about
An old man in a gate hole
Spits into the cobbled backs
And watches a young woman
With a fat behind, pinning
Washing out, in a pair of slacks.

Bernard and John

Bernard and John have gone to Majorca
Their seats in the smoke room are empty.
They usually sit in the same seats each night
They catch the same bus each night
And drink the same quantity of beer each night
Except on a Saturday, when they have a pint extra.
Both are bachelors and likely to remain happily so,
Both are diligent clerks, good workers,
Never have a day off, except tor illness,
Never are late
And never speak ill of their bosses,
Or the political system.
On the matter of sport they do differ slightly,
John likes a flutter on the gee gees
Bernard supports the local football team.
He has a season ticket
And year in, year out, come rain, snow or blizzard
He stands there each Saturday on the terraces.
Each year in early September
They take a continental holiday.
They have been on a cruise to the Greek Islands
And to Los Palmas.
They have been to Austria, Switzerland
And North Africa,
where they remember seeing flies
On the food in the market place, and a woman
Who squatted down in the street and relieved herself.

This caused them some amusement
But they never want to go there again.
In the last few years they have been
Going to Majorca,
To the same hotel each year
And this seems to suit them very well
And they sing its praises.
The hotel has a swimming pool,
But neither of them swim.
It has a ballroom
But neither of them dance.
They also laughingly tell me that there are
A number of available women there,
But neither of them are womanisers.
The hotel is situated a few yards from the sea,
And has a stretch of private beach
With coloured umbrellas,
But neither of them are suited by
Temperament or physique to beach life
So lounging all day three parts naked
In the sun is out.
And that leaves eating
And they speak glowingly of the cuisine
Each day there is a great variety
Of rich foods on the menu
Beef stroganoff, Turkish kebabs, goulash,
Smoked salmon, duckling in honey sauce,
Marvellous many tiered gateaux,
But neither of them is a big eater.

Indeed, Bernard has a small stomach
And has difficulty in polishing off a
Bag of crisps at one go,
And John quickly complains of being distended
By this yearly blow-out at the Hotel Splendide.
But the nearness of all these pleasures pleases them
And during the many evenings
In the smoke room
Throughout the long winter
They reminisce.

Wednesday Night

Last night in the bar of The Leopard
Where I usually call
There was no-one there
No-one at all
Not a single customer
Only a barmaid sitting there
Staring at the empty chairs
On Wednesday it is usually thin
But I'd never before
Known nobody to be in
The place was completely deserted
Not a solitary soul
In either the smoke room
The passage or the bar
Even the man who usually
Sits in the corner chair
Against the sandwich container
Him that is usually
Befuddled by drink
He wasn't there
And he's as regular as clockwork
Digging his grave with a whisky glass
You could set your watch by him
But last night
Even his chair was empty
I have occasionally in the past known nights
That were quiet

But never before
Has there been no-one in
Not a single customer in the house
The beer mats
Were all neatly arranged
On the tables
The ash trays were all cleaned out
And all the stools were placed
Around the polished tables
Evidently where they had been
Neatly arranged
And in the black mahogany front of the piano
The yellow striplights over the bar were reflected
Like a rigid pattern
Of luminous flowers
The barmaid said it was
Getting near to Christmas
And people were beginning to save up
But knowing the bar flies
That frequent the bar I should
Hardly think that this was the
Reason for their absence
No I should think that the explanation
Would more likely to be
Similar to that which causes
Flocks of birds to suddenly all
Change direction at the same time
And then fly off to foreign parts on the same day
Or the reason that children

Take up hula hoops or yoyos
And then just as quick suddenly stop
Cumulative decisions taken separately
By each member of a group
Like a subconscious radar
That for once has left the bar of The Leopard empty
It's either that or they've all suddenly
Decided to become teetotal

The Patriots

I am no radical, no lefty
but then again I don't automatically stand
when the National Anthem's played
I have lived long enough
to know that things always change
but I would rather the change was
slower than fast
I believe there must be a structure
a figurehead
but I'm not crazy about the idea
it doesn't cause the hairs to prickle
on the back of my head
I believe in paying my taxes
but I don't rush to the tax office
with notes in my hand
I think my heart has felt the range of all the normal
        emotions
from cuddly luvvy dovey to living hell
but when I saw the hoy polloi in the inner ring at Ascot
throw their hats in the air when the Queen passed
and shout hurrah, hurrah, hurrah
I thought there must be summat up with me
then I thought there might be summat up with them
something basically different
in their psycho, physio, neurological map
but my eyes work on the same principle as theirs
my nose breathes air in the same way

my heart and pulse are in the same places as theirs
but I could never in a million years
shout hurrah like them
and I got to wondering how it would feel to be shouting it
and why I seem to have missed out
how, for instance, does a man feel
who throws his top hat in the air
and shouts hip hip hooray
on Coronation day
but then I must admit I'm an awkward cuss
It's the same at Christmas
jingle bells don't work for me either
when show biz stars
are cracking jokes and pulling crackers
in the children's ward of local hospitals
watched by sick children in their beds
I have no doubt they are sincere
all the children are laughing
and the Teddy Bears are life size
but for all these toys
and all this sincerity
I have difficulty and draw away
oh, I go for the star, the donkey, the crib
the little Jesus meek and mild bit
but it's the velvet bow ties
I have difficulty with
but even they can be swallowed at a pinch
a bit of tinsel's OK by me
but hurrah, hurrah, hurrah

and they were so whole hearted
you could tell that
and after all a topper's a very expensive hat
but I've always been the same
at parties I never know how to mingle
carrying a cocktail
or a cup of coffee if it comes to that
I've never been able to insinuate
myself into a conversation
and then politely move away
I suppose it's all a matter of
good taste and etiquette
but to throw your hat in the air
and shout hooray
well your feelings must be bursting from you
Hip Hip Hooray
I wonder what it feels like to feel like that

The Irishman

My name is Jack Mulcahy
And I've lost the use of my eye
I lost it one Saturday morning
In a Pub they call the Shanghai
It was a fellah called Casey that struck me
He came at me from behind
And ever since that morning
My left eye has been blind
The bloke it was that hit me
He was as big as the side of a house
And there was no more feeling in him
Than there is in a black haired louse
I left my home in Wicklow
Just before the war
And somehow I don't think dear old Ireland
Will see me any more
I've lifted the pavements in Glasgow
I've dug up the streets of Hull
And I've never left a pub at night
Until I've had my belly full
Once I had a job in Derby
Working for the North Sea gas
I remember it was a Sunday morning
Just after early Mass
I met a man in a bar there
He spoke bad about my race
So I lifted up my fist and smashed him in the face

Then I did a month in Strangeways
Behind the iron bars
I shared a cell while in there
With a man who stole motor cars
Oh there are drunken men and stupid men
And men with minds like goats
And there are men who when they've had a drink
Are quick to take off their coats
From Lime Street to Glasgow Central
From Euston to Waterloo
I've had my share of the Guinness
And I've been drunk a time or two
But I've always paid my lodgings
And tried to keep myself clean
And there's no man living
Who can say Jack Mulcahy's mean.
I've always worked hard for my living
I've dug deep for my daily bread
And as for the matter of drinking
Well bejesus I'll drink deep until I'm dead.

11 p.m.

At this hour of the night
As the drabs and doxies
Of this town
Leave the pubs
They are filled with drink
As they attempt to run across
The road in their tight skirts
And high heeled shoes
They experience some difficulty
But their efforts only seem to
Amuse them,
And cause them to shriek
With vulgar laughter
Their plastic handbags
And coats of coloured artificial fur
Gleam under the neon lights
Some are fat, some are thin
But at any rate
You can be sure
They have all made the most of themselves
And deserve some credit for that
As they trip past
Laughing and giggling
Through the darkness
Toward the brightly lit doorway
Of the local night club
They leave a whiff

Of cheap but pleasant scent
Behind them
It is evident that they are
Very happy
And no doubt look forward
To further pleasures
From the night.

Sad Girl

This morning I saw one
Of the night creatures of this town
Sheltering in a doorway
From the perishing wind.
She is a sort of part time,
Good time, amateur whore.
She had a young child clinging to her
Crying to be lifted up,
But she ignored it
And drew her black skin coat
More closely around her body.
The child continued to torment her
And soon she began to curse
And threaten it.
Her face without her nightmask
Was coloured like clay
And a thin gauze scarf
Held tubular plastic curlers
In place on her head.
No one seeing her there
Would ever guess
That this was the stilt heeled,
Black sheathed, provocative creature
Who at night graced the smoke-rooms
Of notorious public houses
And later could be seen
At the local night clubs

Smiling and mincing
Her tight thighed way
Among this company
Like a sequinned thing,
Sensual, alluring, near and available.
One thing is certain
Cigarette smoke
Suits her better
Than the cold morning wind.

Night

Great gob-eyed loons
Twist their heaving
Ball of gum
From cheek to cheek
Miscagnegated louts
With pimpled faces
Eye the passing dollies
With a surly malevolence
A soft swash thighed thing
No more than fifteen
Screams
As her young nipples
Press through
Her flimsy blouse
Her buttered eyes
Melt in the exhaust fumes
As the roaring Panthers
Pass.

New Year's Eve

The old year's gone, a new beginning
The pubs are full of drunken faces grinning
A bottle smashed, a man is sick
As the town hall clock is heard to tick
Ten, eleven, twelve, the bells are ringing
The streets are full of raucous singing
The lad that saw the old year out
Is nothing but a drunken lout
Who stood and spewed against a wall
And when his mate was seen to fall
Into the water in the gutter
Turned his head and was heard to mutter
Get up yer stupid-looking bugger,
And let us try an' get another drink,
If thay stop'st down there thay't end up in clink.

The Gentlemen's Convenience

At night the light over the steps
That leads down into the gentlemen's convenience
Reminds me of a crucifix
A glass faced crucifix
That shines down the steps
To where a weighing machine
Looks as sad and innocent
As a glass-faced Magdalene
But unfortunately it is out of order
And so is the air purifier
Which has got one of its vents stuck
Clogged up by dirt I should think
In its stillness it resembles a pig's snout
Put there to suck the foul air out
This convenience is usually a well-kept place
The attendant a bronchial man
Takes a great pride in his job
And when it rains
Lays great pieces of cardboard
Over the floor to absorb the
Wet footmarks from the street
But unfortunately he is ill at home
Propped up in bed trying to get his breath
And his place has been taken by a
Bleary wide-eyed man
Who resents doing the job
And never pokes his head out of

The small room
Where there is a gas fire, a table and a teapot
And a cupboard where the mops, the buckets and the
Lavatory paper are kept
He sits in there studying the racing papers all day
It is evident he is only there for the pay
And has no regard for the rituals and mysteries
Of this holy convenience at all

In the Gents

Above the angle
Of the damaged roof light
Above the edge of the Public house wall
Over the top of the gentlemen's lavatories
Beyond the corrosion of pipes
And the decaying of cisterns
Above the erotic scratches on the wall
Through the glare of the neon lit sign from the
      Bingo Palace
As I stand piddling in the crazed urinal stall
I can see the red and green tail lights
Of some night plane
Moving across this area of infinite velvet
Over the darkened hoop of the world.

Pleasure Meter

If there was a meter to measure pleasure
what reading would it give, I wonder.
Would a bacon sandwich measure
as high as the love light in your eye
or sherry trifle mean as much as kisses
or beef dripping — however could you
hope to compete with that?
Or pigs head, brawn for that matter
and vanilla ice cream would surely
be the equal of love's young dream.
Fresh garden peas just out of their pods
are food I think fit for the gods.
Your charms I think would stand a chance
against two rounds of toast
or a pork pie or a piece of cheese.
Against such pleasures as these
you may be able to compete.
Yes, I think your arms, your hair,
your shapely thighs
would stand a good chance
against most pork pies
but I can't be really sure
which I like the best.
I wish I had a pleasure meter
to put you to the test.

A Lost Love

Once I gave my love a flower
she held it to her nose
but she found its smell obnoxious
and said it didn't match her clothes
such clothes she had
nothing but the best
her wardrobe was as big as a pantechnicon
Then I gave her an apple
I'd found on the floor
when I told her where I'd found it
she threw it through the door
she said that fallen apples
would be covered in deadly germs
and should be left where they'd fallen
to be eaten by birds and worms
Her temper was as fierce as a blow torch
she had no time for fools
when I said that to err was human
she replied that rules were rules
so I gave her a fly spray
to kill the buzzing flies
but she hardly ever used it
she said it got into her eyes
and that the spray was poison
and should by law be banned
as the filthy stuff within it
was poisoning the land

The thought she gave to public matters
it quite put me to shame
when I said the fault was the government's
she said we'd only got ourselves to blame
Oh, my love was very hygienic
she bathed at least once a day
and blew her nose on paper tissues
one day she blew it so fiercely
she blew my love away

Advice to a Young Man

A young man should beware
His life is in danger
From women with black moustaches
And hair growing on their legs
These women are always
Very passionate and demanding
And when their soft tongues
Touch their white teeth
And their breasts press
Urgently against him
In the darkness
And they whisper in his ear
He should try to remember
That they will
Not be satisfied
Until they have
Filled his life with squealing children.
He should also avoid
Hawk nosed girls
With over active glands
Whose eyes stare wildly
And whose thin fingered hands
Gesticulate
And may wander and excite
Him with quick fierce intensity
These women become goiterous
Later in life

And constantly whine
About their missed chances
Avoid too, bored girls
Their boredom will run deep
Right into the very centre of
Their souls,
It is incurable,
And it will crucify their days
With a constant stream of sighs
Wishing for this, or wishing for that
There is no way of satisfying
Their endless whims.
But more than these,
Far more,
Avoid like the plague
Women with tattoos on their arms
No matter what their other charms,
These women have tempers wilder
Than a North Sea wind
And would gladly smash a window
If their will is crossed
A man in their clutches
Might as well give in
Or pack his bags
And steal away in the night
And take a back room in Kilburn
Or Camden Town, and lie low for a long time.
But God help him if he's ever found
He'll get no more peace till he's in the ground

Prattle

Do you like the colour of my hair
Would you rather it was dark
Or would you like it fair
Or say ash blonde for a change
Do you like the colour of my eyes
Do you think they match my clothes
And do you care for painted toes
Or would you rather I left them plain
And free from any stain just natural
Oh don't be a bore
I think I'm really rather nice don't you
Especially from the left side view
I have rather a distinguished nose don't you think
And my hands are long and elegant
That's why I keep away from the sink
And other heavy chores
Does my figure please you
I have never seen the back view
What am I really like from the back
Oh I wish I was by the sea
Lying on the sand
With a bottle of sun tan lotion
Being massaged into my skin
Oh I wish I had a new fur coat
Musquash or better still mink
That ghastly creature Sally is demented
I can understand her husband taking to drink

I hear her daughter's on the Pill
I am not a bit surprised
Did you see the look in her eyes
I wonder what she sees in him
Or him in her for that matter
She's always filled with such idle chatter
And she's such a snob
She makes me sick
Always on about what she's got
She was as poor as a church mouse
Till she met him
I could tell you a thing or two
Her language at times can turn the air blue
What's the matter with you
Don't sit there pulling your face
Count yourself lucky you haven't
Got some women
God I get so bored at times I could scream
Oh darling let me tell you about my dream
I dreamt that as put on my new fur coat
Something horrible crept up
And grabbed me by the throat

Love Is

Love is much mouthed
much sung about
it is sprayed silver on walls
scrawled on the back of lavatory doors
carved on trees
hooligans have it tattooed on their fingers
it has an easy currency
it sings songs, sells songs,
makes songs if it comes to that
they say it is sincere
they say it is true
but they also say it is blind
it is also associated with the moon
and the stars
and sometimes it is found at the end of a rainbow
but it is also unfortunately true
that it often dies
and then there are more songs made about it
sad songs, but good songs
for sadness does make good songs
in fact, the best love songs are sad songs
I have also seen it break windows
cut throats, make men take poison
drive them mad
love is also often held in silence
and sometimes you don't know
it's been there till it's gone

No Jackpot

There is no jackpot here
These coloured machines
Give no prizes,
No dreams come true,
No small fortunes
They promise nothing.
Their only bonus
Is the chance to play again
Under the same conditions.
The bright steel ball
Is propelled by a spring
That is pulled by the player,
One thousand,
Two thousand,
Three thousand,
Twelve? the bell rings
The springs light the lights
That flash quickly on and off,
Off and on,
All over the various paths
The steel ball can make
Among the apparently endless
Permutations and possibilities
Open to it.
I feel I must repeat
These coloured machines
Give no prizes

No dreams come true,
No small fortunes
They promise nothing
No matter how the coloured lights
Seem to disguise it.
Their hardest reward
Is merely the chance
To play again for
Exactly the same stakes
Till the arm aches
Or until the heart is broken
From its hoping
And at last
Can play the game for its own sake.
There is no jackpot here.

Stone Walls and Privet Hedges

Among these next poems there are bits of green sprouting, a few leaves here and there. Some of them are generated by the moorland landscape which is a tribal thing to me. Scrawn hill farms and stone walls and scaly legged old hens are a deep part of my nature. Brown Edge, Smallthorne, Nettlebank, Lask Edge, Biddulph Moor, this is the country that calls to me. Thin soiled places where men worked in the pits and kept a stirk or two, a Primitive Methodist landscape where clogs struck what sparks there were and winter is perishing and all the folks keep their money under their beds.

Rustic Memory

Long ago
in a hot summer
I went into a little slanting field
to help with the mowing
there were other boys there
drinking pop
monkeying about
or lying there
sprawled against
the bales of hay or straw
there was also a man
with a pikel
he was smoking
I remember noticing the smoke
was a different colour
from the hay
the man wore braces and a belt
it was the first time
I realised the sun was yellow

Bus Window

A shelf of slanting rock fractures the earth,
The thin soil of the moor
Still shows the white wounds of snow.
Low walls huddle their stones
At the back of the high road.
A thin wind blows
As a scaly legged old barnevelder fowl
Pecks among the gorse.
By a telegraph pole stands a lonely horse.
Stirks shelter from the wind,
Their soft muzzles press the rotting gate.
An old man standing in the door of a barn
Slowly raises his arm
To shade his eyes
From the fierce light of the skies
As the afternoon bus passes by.

The Church School

The church school
has got a bell tower but no bell
It used to have a bell
With a miserable clank
But thieves stole it one weekend
Along with lead from the church roof
The police caught the thieves
But it was too late
The bell had been broken up
And sold as scrap
The church school
Had a boiler that often burst
And sometimes in winter
The church school was a very cold school
And the pupils had to sit in their coats
The church school desks were very old
And were scratched and gouged
With names of pupils who had
Long since left
These church school desks
Had moulded iron legs and tip up seats
And when the big boys' hobnailed boots
Clashed on these iron legs it caused a terrible clatter
And drove the teachers mad
There was one teacher called Mr Whympenny
He was the deputy head
His real head was quite bald

Except for a little fringe of white hair
Around the edge
This made his head look like
A big egg in a nest
He also wore a cardigan
And polished his shoes every day
And always made the children
Stand to attention before they went out to play
The playground of the church school was very small
Surrounded by thick iron railings on top of the walls
Each of these railings had a spike on the top
To stop the pupils climbing over
One boy once climbed over and a spike stuck in him
None of the children climbed over since then
The church school had lavatories in the yard
Where the big boys went to have a smoke
Some of the boys smoked under the bike shed
Where them as had got them left their bikes
Inside the church school
It smelled of soft soap
which was used to keep the school clean
By Mr Sillitoe the caretaker
Who all the children called Cheesy
I don't know why they called him this
I think the name must have been handed down
In the hall of the church school
There were a lot of pegs
Where the children hung their little peg bags
For putting their pumps in

All the bags had children's names
Crocheted on in chain stitch
Above the bags there was a
Big coloured map of the world stuck on the wall
Showing all the foreign lands
At the side of the map
There is a picture of the King under a union jack

Winter

I saw winter today
in a field of mangolds
standing by a wet stone wall
he was acting the goat
and had sucked a marrow bone empty
to use as a flute
the tune he played
sounded to me like the
rattle of phlegm
but it drove the crows wild
and made the sow pigs squeal
then when he cracked his finger bones
and tried to wipe the
sockets of his eyes
with a handful of dead leaves
I noticed
how curious his ribs were hinged
one moved sideways
and another broken by the wind
flanged inwards
and as it moved
I caught a glimpse of his heart
it was an old crow's nest
fastened by a shaft of dead hair
it was then I knew
he was mad
and would sometime

try to destroy me
as death was his favourite sport
after all he had once
played a bloated bagpipe
and ridden a grey horse
in the biggest regiment in the world
the regiment of skeletons

Poem for my Father

There is a man
With icicles on his hat
Who passes my house each day.
The bleak winds
Do not offend him.
Stone walls
Have stiffened his blood.
Sometimes he carries
A piece of wood
Under his arm,
A broken branch
To light his fire.
He comes from the moors
Where the soil is sparse.
There are sacks
Stuck in his broken windows.
Slit winds
Blow his hens sideways.
His tree is the hawthorn
His flower is the dog rose.
On the altar of his chapel
There are three daffodils
In a jar.
The only time
I ever saw him smile
Was when the world was white
And swollen with snow,

And his young dogs raced
Yelping over
The wet fields
After the mocking peewits.

October Poem

A wet wind sags
And bends the dry stalks
Down to where
The cores of
Sour green apples
Lie among the
Long grass
Round the backs
Old sacks
Nailed in the windows
Of forgotten stables
Flap like wild flags
The damp knees
In the trousers
Of cold youths
Cling to their legs
As the narrow tyres
Of their racing bicycles
Leave thin tracks
On the paths
Thick with wet leaves
Bright points of light
Ride the quick ripples
In the rain
Swollen pond
Moving, and dancing
In luminous patterns
To merge with the blinding light of the water burnished sun.

Lament for The Lump of Coal

The public house known as The Lump of Coal is closed
    forever
The Brewery have sold it for fifteen thousand pounds
The brass handle on the tap room door has been
    unscrewed
and with the bar pumps and the wooden squab from the
    snug
sold as a job lot for little or nothing
the iron legged tables from the smoke room
are stacked in the back yard
and the greenhouse that stood by the whitewashed urinal
has been dismantled and carted off
even the oak beam from which a publican
sodden in drink
hung himself years ago has been sold
to make a fireplace in a solicitor's bungalow I am told
everything is to be changed
the stone wall under the hawthorn hedge
where the colliers
used to sit in summer
and the red quarries the cool red quarries by the back door
where the whippets lay out of the sun
all are being dug up
The Lump of Coal was the last public house
between the pit and the moor
perched high on an outcrop of rock
between a wood of fir trees and Stake Gutter Farm

even in summer there was always a wind blowing
and in winter it often blew so hard
you could hear it down the smoke room chimney
like a muffled roar
this ale house was licensed for singing and music
and was very lively betimes
it was in the smoke room here
the old Ale and Bacca band drank their barrel of beer
won for playing non stop up Blackie Bank
and in the smoke room every Sunday night
Mr Sylvanus Plimbley, a local preacher gone to the bad
would sing "No Rose in All the World" with tears in his
    eyes
while outside at good times
an old box and
rake collier called Thick Finger Jack
would dance and
rattle his clogs on the cellar door
at the same time playing Rule Britannia on
a fiddle made from a corn beef tin
this man had one leg, but such was his resource
he made himself a wooden one with a window
hinge for the knee
it was men like these and such as these
that did their drinking in this stone house
it is their ghosts that will lament its closing most
and somehow I think whoever buys it
will at nights have very troubled sleep

The Chaddocks

Mr. Enoch Chaddock
Known as "Nocky"
Farmed Stakegutter Farm
Forty-seven acres
Of thin soiled hill ground
He was a frugal man
And he worked from
Morning till night
And never spent a penny
The only pleasure he had
Was an occasional bottle of pop
He had only one tooth
And this always seemed to have
A bit of pig meal stuck to it
Which caused him to suck and spit
All the time
It was said he kept his
Money hidden under the floorboards
As he didn't understand banks
His wife Poll
Was a bony woman
As strong as a man
Her greatest pleasure
Was taking milk out
To the fag smoking housewives
On the nearby housing estate
She was a great talker

And when in full flow
Her fierce need to tell her tale
Would make her spit and stutter
She also wore square-toed clogs
Neither she nor her husband
Had ever seen the sea
They had one child
A son called Enoch
After his father
This Enoch was long and thin
And wore an old cap of his father's
Pulled down to his eyebrows
He could not speak
Only grunt
And sometimes not
Even that
His greatest pleasure
Was also hidden under
The floorboards of his bedroom
It was a picture book
With pictures of
Naked women on every page
He had been to the seaside once
On a bus trip to New Brighton
With the British Legion Club
And had found the picture book
Under a seat on the bus

Enoch Adshead

Aged 5 Years
Drowned Whit Monday 1901
IN MEMORIAM

Mrs Selina Adshead
Of Childerplay Farm, Lask Edge
Had a room in her head.
In it was a basket chair
And a marble topped washstand,
And a double bed.
She also had a farm yard in her heart,
A yard with a shippon, a stable,
And a broken cart.
Besides these things
She often had a dream
Of a long barge boat
With painted flowers
On its cabin doors
And a red bucket
And a little dog that barked and barked
As the barge
Passed a herd of cows
The barge was filled with little children
In their best frocks
And sailors suits, and straw hats
And the noise of their play
Filled her dream
Until they came to a tunnel
When she always awoke with a scream

Hill Farm

The sky's a weighted womb of snow
The colour of a darkening pearl
The wind begins to moan and blow
As the drifts begin to shift and swirl
The hedge is black and stiff and stark
Oil lamps are lit against the dark
And in the farm yard on the hill
Icicles form on the window sill

The Blackbird

The old blackbird waits
It can feel the first
Thin steel whistles of winter
Its claws grip the branch
As the tree trembles
And makes the undersides of leaves
A metallic silver glitter
Against the sky.
As the wind's cold razors
Blow the dead leaves by
The old bird blinks
And remembers the demented sky
When young birds huddled
In their flooded nests
Their feather spines whitened
By the pitiless rain
The nights of slow frost
A stiff world of pain
As the blackbird waits
Its eyes are filled
With old birds' fates
They blink in panic
As it waits and waits.

The Swilling Woman

Once I knew a woman who swilled a lot
she was fat but busky with it
never still
every day she got up
she would swill, swill, swill
her house was small and damp
with a floor made of square stone flags
and the clothes she wore
all seemed made of pig meal bags
but she could swill
oh, how she could swill
she swilled that stone floor
six or more times every day
she'd swill it first then
mop the swilled water away
she'd swill, swill, swill
ten times a day if she could
but all this swilling was
doing her husband no good
he'd sit by the door
a bag of rheumatic bones
with his poor slippered feet
just touching the damp, swilled stones
a poor helpless thing he sat there
huddled up in his rocking chair
you'd have thought his condition
would have caused her to stop

but no, she was merciless with
her bucket and mop
get your big feet out of the road
she'd shout
and the old man would do his best to comply
and then with a fierce look in her eye
with nostrils flanged and fists
clenched tight
she'd grasp the bucket handle with all her might
and flood the stone flags once again
and then jaw clenched with bulldog will
She'd swill, swill, swill and swill
till the tiny cottage floor was like a tide
there was no place for anything to hide
not a speck of dust from her old tom cat's tail
could survive the deluge from her pail
six times a day she'd swill at least
and it it happened to be a religious day or a feast
she'd make a special effort to swill six times more
until it seemed she'd wear out the floor
but the stone flags on the floor were very hard
and every year grew harder still
harder even than the swilling woman's will to swill
the old man it was that went the first
one Whit Monday it was, his heart could stand no more
and he fell face first on to the cottage floor
but seeing him there just caused her to swill a few times
    more
and for years after he was put in the ground

she went on with her swilling round
singing to herself as she plied the mop
I thought her swilling would never stop
but swilling women are not made of stone
but softer stuff called flesh and bone
that after a while wears away
and even though she would have
swilled a million times or more
came a day even she could swill no more

Bad Thoughts About Pigeons

I am a man much taken by birds.
Each Saturday I buy wild bird seed.
I did not think it possible
that I could think badly of them
but somehow the wild pigeons have managed it.
Only they are not so wild,
neither for that matter are they tame.
They are somewhere in between
and very fat at that,
like plump dowagers without corsets.
They waddle about or flutter
from the garage to the chimney
where they sit awhile
rather bored and restless.
Then they fly back and
peck about the coalhouse
until the door opens or a dog barks.
Then they make a show
of being alarmed
and ruffle their feathers.
These indolent dollops
will only eat bird seed
and flirt pieces of crust about
as though it wasn't worth the pecking.
Then they bully-bird the sparrows away
and, with an effort,
bloated with wet bread

they just about manage
to raise themselves
off the ground and perch on the guttering
to wait impatiently
for the next hand-out.

Mrs Treacle

In the village that used to be
There was a single street
A post box
A few cottages
And a public house
Called THE LOCOMOTIVE
It was so called because
There used to be
A single track coal line
That ran through
A cutting filled with foxgloves nearby
In the public house
Was a small tap room
A smoke room
And a snug
In the snug there was a small table
That had once been
A sewing machine
But the treadle had been removed
Leaving only the table top
The snug was such a little room
It would only hold four people
At a pinch
And each evening a fat woman
Called Mrs Treacle
Used to sit at this table
And drink a milk stout

Mrs Treacle laid people out
And she kept a few
Old scaly legged hens
That strutted around her
Front door cadging bits of bread
She also had a cock
And as a boy I was terrified of this bird
And each week I went to collect
Her four and tuppence rent
I had to muster all my courage
To pass this fierce bird
Outside Spout Cottage as
Her home was called
There was a spring of cold water
That ran down the stones
All the year round and never stopped
The water was so cold
I can feel it now
It felt cold enough to skin your teeth
I remember Mrs Treacle's rent book was pink
A washed-out faded rent book pink
I always signed my name in it with a
Stub of black lead
The lead was always blunt and thick
And was always put back on the mantleshelf
By the tea caddy
That stood by a photograph
Of Mrs Treacle's only son Jess
Who had been killed years ago

Serving as a soldier in the war in France
The photograph had faded
From a sepia brown
Until it was now nearly yellow
The sun from the small window
Shone on the photo each day
And the sun fades old photographs
And memories away

Easter

There used to be a sort of boredom
Particular to bank holidays
The shops were shut
The buses went past less frequently
On the holiday of the crucifixion
The day of the wooden cross
The day the wounds were made with nails
The boredom could be
A crucifying thing in itself
But happily this seems to be getting less so
Most shops nowadays seem to remain open
People seem to want to get out and about
The main road to the sea
Passes through most people's back windows
And a constantly moving stream
Of small cars can be seen
Driving off to the favourite holiday resorts
For those who stay at home
There are many holiday attractions
The smiling announcers announce
A full programme of sport
Horse jumping, tennis, swimming
All that sort of thing
To pass the day away
Pleasantly entertained
As for the other business
The Man of Nazareth seems to be losing out

The crown of thorns
Is lost among the motor horns
A constant reminder of unpleasant things
Wounds, thorns, blood and death,
Who wants constantly to be reminded
Of these grim realities
The world is full enough of suffering
As it is, and as for
Vicarious atonement, love, that is
The two halves of the world
Are ready to get at each other's throats
Over what it means.

Contrast

Contrast the weariness
Of school teachers
After their work
With the wildness
Of young workmen
In the back of lorries
Pinching a ride
Leaping over the side
Laughing and gambling
In huts on building sites
Opening racing papers
Drinking from tin mugs
Among the big breasted pin-ups
Their white teeth filled with
Laughing obscenities
It makes you wish you were
A builder's labourer
But not in winter when
There is ice on the bricks.

A Fly in the Ointment

The new Municipal Library
in the High Street
is where the old Municipal Hall
and the dog pound used to be
The Council have really gone to town on the building
it is most handsome
there's a different coloured felt carpet on each floor
and an elegant staircase
leading to the reference rooms on the second floor
a place where quiet and prolonged study is possible
with separate cubicles
each with a click on light
in the main body of the Library
where the Library books are
there is a wonderful clockwork clock
it must be all of ten feet high
you can see all the works working
and the big fingers give a quiet but firm tick tock
as they move round the clockface
it is a marvel of nineteenth century engineering
and then there are the toilets
these are the twentieth century at its best
the lavatories are so splendid one might sit there
and easily imagine you were in a first class hotel
all the fitments are polished aluminium
even the toilet rolls are of high quality
you get to these palatial lavatories by means

of a small steel lift with flashing lights
that move up and down to let you know exactly
where you are – outside the lift on the ground floor
there is a telephone kiosk made in the shape of a plastic
    dome
the sort you see on the television in films about New York
the whole place is so up to date and tasteful with it
it is a pleasure and a thrill to go in
and all the library assistants seem to appreciate it
they are very beautiful these assistants, not only neat and
    tidy
young women in cardigans as one might expect library
    assistants to be
but stilt heeled slim bloused beauties
whose satin blouses ripple over their firm young breasts
it is very difficult to concentrate on choosing a book
if one of them happens to be near you
in that part of the library where the non-fiction books are
there are great tall windows facing the High Street
and through these one can see the passing parade
and the library have arranged
two elegant and comfortable armchairs
facing the window
it is most civilised and a calming experience to sit on one
of these chairs and spend an hour browsing
but unfortunately there is a fly in the ointment
each day that ever comes as regular as the clockwork
    clock
sitting there in one of the armchairs like a gentlemen
is a local tramp who has found the new library to his liking

and sits from morning to night reading cheap cowboy
stories
he is everything the library is not
his hair sticks out matted with
what looks like pigeon droppings
he looks like a wild man, a human yak
his flyhole is fastened with a safety pin
and he has a piece of string round his waist in lieu of a
belt
and worse than this his shoes or what is left of them
disclose his filthy toenails to the public view
it is a certain fact that when he is sitting in his chair
there is no-one sitting in the other
as the stench of dry urine
and the sound of him snuffling phlegm
soon drives them away
the young library assistants look at him with disgust
as he sits gnawing at a piece of rough crust he has no
doubt
filched from some ash bin
and what is worse, if one of them approaches him
he gives them a stare of such malevolence and mumbles
obscenities just under his breath that
they, not wishing to be involved
in an altercation with such a creature
give him a wide berth
The head librarian, a woman who seems to have
an air purifying system halfway up her nose
says that it's a disgrace
that such a creature should be allowed in the place

and that the council should provide homes for such
 people
the bearded one seems to agree with her
as he lies sprawled there he's like a gentleman
in his municipal armchair

The Caretakers

The Public Institute is heavy with
The spirits of bygone caretakers.
They meet you in the vestibule
Under the busts of the benefactors.
They are uneasy about their
Lost responsibilities.
Their presence admonishes.
I can feel them sternly watching
The men who gaze at nothing
In the Public Reading Room.
I can hear their heavy tread
Up the main staircase
That leads from the entrance hall
And then sub-divides into
Separate symmetrical routes
To the upper corridors.
Their lives were crucified
On these stairs
That once led to the rooms
Filled with stuffed birds
And boxes of butterflies.
There was an owl with a
Mouse in its beak here
And a great eagle with a snake
And a sea bird of some kind
With a fish.
All very interesting.

This still world was always
To the caretakers liking
it was quiet and unmoving
Except for the reflections.
All this, of course was before
The building was used
As an educational centre.
After that it was all very different.
First the birds disappeared
And then the glass cases
Were smashed and disposed of
And the rooms were filled
With mining apprentices
Who scratched obscenities
On the lavatory walls
And threw paper drinking cups
Over the balcony
And broke the coffee vending machine
From its brackets.
The coming of these mobs
Drove the caretakers to a despair
From which they never recovered
And one by one they either
Handed in their resignation
Or disappeared
To lick their wounds
Down the cellar steps
That lead to the boiler room.

A Comfortable Old Age

On a dreary Sunday afternoon
In a detached Victorian villa
At the end of the avenue
In the front room
Under a print of tea roses
And a church calendar
Two white haired old ladies
Are watching their favourite
Television quiz programme
They are eating liqueurs
A present from last Christmas
As they slice the tops off
The little chocolate bottles
With their false teeth
Their 'pussy boy' stretches
In his basket
By the window.

Wrong Category

There was this man
Who walked his dog
Round the pond each
Day at the same time.
I never spoke to him
Nor him to me.
He was a clerkly
Looking man
With horn rimmed spectacles,
A sort of English Japanese.
A very sedentary
Sort of person,
A manager's man,
Very reserved
Much concerned with his rights.
A good servant
With a strong sense of property,
And propriety.
His main emotion
Was a slight annoyance
HIs dog was a
Yapping poodle called Pepi,
Pepi, Pepi, come here Pepi,
He shouted after it
In vain each day.
The dog was disobedient
And pleased itself

It irritated me to hear him.
I had got him into the right category
I was sure
And had dismissed him,
Until one day in Autumn
As I sat on the park seat
Watching the leaves float
On the pond
For the first time
He stopped, and
Passed the time of day
And stood watching
The leaves on the water
For a moment,
And then he commented
That the floating leaves
Were shaped like the barges
Of ancient Egypt
That floated down the Nile,
And sure enough,
When I looked at them
Closely, they did.

A Salute

As I passed the park tonight
I suddenly remembered
A man I had completely forgotten
A Romanian or Hungarian
Modeller of tigers
I remember he always wore a homburg
And had a touch of gold about him
A gold tooth, a gold signet ring
I have noticed that Slavonic people
Have a liking for gold
He also had a Pomeranian dog
Which was very disobedient and often strayed
But having short legs it couldn't wander far
He told me he modelled tigers in his parlour
Sometimes he modelled elephants
But mostly tigers as they were very popular
And looked very handsome
When they were glazed with rouge flambé
A deep blood-red glaze that melts into black
He had been trained as a student
In Munich under Professor Lieble
Fritz Lieble was an artist
Who painted Bavarian women
Kneeling and praying in church
In a very realistic style
Each detail in the women's dress
Being minutely observed

And the Slavonic modeller of tigers
Was warm in his praise of such work
And had no sympathy with
Work of a less precise nature
For years we had passed the time of day
Beside the lake in the park
Him walking very slowly
As I believe he was suffering from
Some kind of vascular disease
For which his doctor had prescribed tablets
That thinned his blood
His legs often pained him a great deal
And this would account for the
Slow and deliberate way
He walked round the paths
Our acquaintance was such
That I might not see him
For weeks without noticing it
But I remember that a thought
About not seeing him had
Crossed my mind
Then one day I passed his house
And I noticed that the blinds were drawn
And so were the blinds of his neighbours
I never saw him again
And so as I pass the park tonight
I salute and apologise
For forgetting you
Slavonic modeller of rouge flambé tigers

The Apple Tree

Each year that I have lived in this house
That dry and twisted stem of wood
Standing in the middle of the garden
Has produced a crop of sour apples
But as the house is on the main road
And many children pass
In full view of the apple tree
I always collect the fruit before it ripens
So as not to tempt them
To trespass on my property
When I collect these unripe apples
I put them in a cardboard carton
Such as one may get
From any grocer's shop
And give them to a man who keeps pigs
At the back of my mother's Council house.
My mother is now over seventy years of age
And I cannot get to see her as often
As would like
And as the pigman has a telephone
Sometimes I ring a message through to him
And he passes it on to her
The apples are a present to him
For this service.
As he feeds his pigs mostly
On old bread and swill
A few sour apples will cause his sows to slobber

And I feel satisfied
That I have protected my property
Kept in touch with my mother
And I am sure,
Pleased the pigs.
Apple tree,
I salute you.

False Hopes

All the birds seem to have got the wrong idea
They think the winter's over and spring is here
The first warm wind for months caused this confusion
And filled their wet feathers with this illusion
That the frost is gone and the pain is over
And that from now on in they'd be in clover
I'm afraid they're in for a nasty shock
The frost is gone but will soon be back
With dreadful nights that will do for some
For there's nearly half of the winter yet to come.

Cats

If all the kittens
Our cats once had
Grew into cats
By now they would have
Found their way to London
And in the tall white houses
Round the squares
Distinguished men
Passing on the stairs
Would say to each other
With some concern
Where are all these
Damn cats coming from?

The Blossom

It was altogether too sudden
A shock quite unexpected
The power of it
Exploding its foam overnight
And nearly as quickly gone
Too direct an approach
To loveliness
To happiness,
The simply gorgeous
Overwhelmed
The neat and temperate garden
The avenue was stunned
Surely a miracle
Out of context
It could not last.
When the damp petals fell
On the pavement
In the late cold winds of May
And blew away
Among the exhaust fumes
Things quickly got back
To normal again.

The Blossom Blown, c1990s

The Fall

Since the new road intersection opened
It has made a noticeable difference to the traffic
Now there are three blockages between
Here and the town
First the roundabout
Then the lollipop man who stands
In front of the infants' school
Then the crossroads and the cross
The morning was frosty
And the windows of the cars were misted up
And the drivers were impatient
As we approached the intersection I could see from
The left hand window
The grey silhouette of the distant steel works
Partly obliterated by strange pinkish steam clouds
The other window it was also misty
So I cleared an arc with my fingers
And stared out at the big noticeboard
On the waste ground between the road and the station
And for a moment my attention was taken
By the image of a pregnant man
Feeling his stomach and looking alarmed
This poster was an attempt by the government
To make people more aware of
The responsibilities of bringing children into the world
In a moment we were past the noticeboard
And it was then I saw him

Saw the man that fell
I could see at once there was something wrong
There was a woman with him
He was half sitting on a wall
And she was bending down and speaking to him
Touching him, trying to help him
I could see that she was concerned
But his body was at an angle and he couldn't seem to
hear her
Then he began to fall sideways
I had seen a big chimney fall
And he fell in that way
Not like a man falls
Bending to break his fall
But he fell stiff and rigid
And I noticed his face was red, very red
Seconds later he was lying flat
Parallel with the bottom of the wall
And the pavement
And for a second I wondered what it felt like to fall
Suddenly to have some organ collapse inside you
And in public to be flat and helpless under the sky
When I looked again we had driven a
Few yards past and couldn't stop
As all the traffic behind would have been blocked

Portrait

The face gave no apparent indication
As to the general character of the person observed
It was a face that could mean anything
Could go in any number of directions
As it was deeply confused at the root
Of its being
By the illusion of its own possibilities
It had become nervous of itself
How could it have any courage at all
When it had not the courage of its own convictions
When it was confused as to what those convictions were
In the first place
It was defeated at the start by its own seeming diversity
After so many false starts and hopes
That this was the right way at last
Had been dashed by a sudden change of heart
The only thing that it was sure about was this
That all its sudden enthusiasms, fevers, desires
Would all dissolve as soon as they had come
Oh, the nose, the eyes, the mouth,
The usual features were there in the right places
But they did not add up to any sort
Of definite character at all
At another time, maybe, the matter would have been
    much simpler
The economics of another century
Would not have allowed such a thing to occur

But this would perhaps have been better
Than being impaled by its own apparent freedom
Imprisoned by it in fact
By the very act of choosing
Fixed forever in a flux
Unable to commit oneself right to the very end
The gifts are set against each other
One the father, one the mother.

The Telephone Message

Will you wait a moment please, hold the line
As you stand there stopped in time
Your will presses against the metal edges
Your eyes stare into the looking glass
Time hangs loose, no use
Drum your fingers on the coin box
And listen to the delicate tick of your wristwatch
These dumb waits are implacable
How the seconds stretch waiting there
The tongue touches a sore and pulpy spot
And all the comings and goings
That led you to this edge
Are turning over and over while you wait
Holed up in this place, this barren waiting place
Unable to force yourself forward
To press into your unlived life
A repeated note, they are not at home
Raw serrations of altered situations
What's the use
The moment and the desire will never fuse
The unsatisfactory compromises
Have set hard making it useless
To go back to the original intention
Better to settle for what you can get
The question of a moment of decision is absurd
This kiosk is strongly constructed
To withstand the attacks of hooligans

In the mirror I watch my mouth
The lines around my mouth
I can see the weakness trapped
By the lines that have lived them out
Sorry to keep you waiting sir
There doesn't seem to be any reply sir

The Road to Nowhere

It seems a reasonable supposition
On the face of It
A sensible conclusion
Given a certain attitude of mind
But,
The problem divides as one examines it
Into what one would imagine
Might become another proposition entirely
It's all a matter of degree really
That is,
When you boil it down
To its essentials
In fact
It's always the same problem
A constantly changing equation
That subdivided into secondary categories
That in themselves seem
Rapidly to change
And to defy definitive calculations
As though
The mind could not hold it
In centre for long enough
To reach a decision
One way or the other
The question could not be answered
Anyway. So why ask it?
I think the trouble is

You have not got enough to occupy your mind.
You want to watch out
You'll end up in queer street
It isn't worth it
Believe me I know.

The New Regime

It is not possible to avoid the inevitable
It seems inexorable
That things move in the directions
That they do
The new managers were appointed
Because of their greater efficiency
The old owners were for the most part
Glad to be put out to grass
Well compensated of course
They put up a bit of a fight
But when the wisest of them saw the light
The others soon followed
These new men have different faces
Or at least it seems so
When you see them looking out
From the broad mesh of a newspaper photograph
Smiling genially or looking appropriately serious
Just as the occasion demands
Their faces look so reasonable
It is hard to imagine the stories
Of their ruthlessness being true
The chief henchmen of the old regime
Are those that tremble most
The new masters want a different kind
Of hatchet man
More sophisticated you might say
Their dirty work must be done in a different way

If the business is to pay
And so the good servants
The old right hand men
Tremble, as they await
Their fate
They bitterly complain
That they were born too late
New brooms sweep clean
You know what I mean
It's all so different
Under the new regime.

Sad Office Thoughts

If only I could fall back again
To the place where my cheek was
Cool against the damp splintered wood
And my mouth was filled with the bitter taste
        of orange peel
And liquorice root
Before I had wounded each day with my worrying
When all my wounds could be counted on
My knees, or on the cut fingers
Of my hands. If I could leap
Above my salary scales
And burn the endless rate bills
And leave the dreadful reasonableness
Of my well meaning colleagues
And cut through the Institution's lies
If only my eyes had been set a little farther apart
And my brow had been calmer
If only my narrow lungs
Could have opened wide enough to have held
A little more wind
And my mind had not stumbled over so many pebbles
And comforted itself with sighs
Then perhaps I should have been able to
Count some profit from all these years
Instead of this, the more I live the more I miss.

Additional Poems

Town Hall in January

Fine snow in the teeth of the wind
Blows under the Town Hall doors
The waiting bus queues huddle closer together.
Women whine, "The bus is a long time
In coming." A hunchback, a cripple foot
Shuffles in at the door
Of the Public Reading Room,
Where the head of a sleeping man rests
On a shining table, slipped down
In the oblivion of his dreams.
Pockets of life, of half life
Slide uneasily by
Their irretrievable faces hide
Behind magazines
As the mindless wind explodes
In its furious ends.
From the windows the old men watch
The thickening sky.
High up above in the gathering gloom
The statue of an angel holds up
A laurel wreath, to the slate grey clouds
Where, barely discernible in fading light
Under the angel's armpit, against its bronze wing
The white shape of a town hall pigeon
Can be seen fluttering.

The following poem was written to accompany and explain the painting *The Good Son* when it was shown as part of Arthur Berry's retrospective exhibition at the City Museum and Art Gallery, in 1984.

The Good Son, 1973

The Old Woman's Tale

Nobody knows nobody knows
how good our Stanleys been to me
has been unknown good
hes one of the best lads ever to
    tread shoe leather Stan is
he's a damn sight different than
                our Elsie
her'd have had me in a old folks home
                years ago
if we ever been short of a shilling
hes always got his hand in his pocket
hes as good as gold our Stan is
and always has been
through thick and thin
         thick and thin
and I can tell you theres
         been a lot of thin
nobody knows nobody knows

What I Paint and How As Best I Can

I paint   men
    especially
        men's heads
  men walking
        some sitting
  I paint women
        and girls often
            naked
  I paint rooms
        often empty
    to paint their emptiness
  I paint bottles and apples
    and cake stands
    because they are
  simple and have
      richness and
        dignity
  I paint houses   and
            bungalows
   roads
  and walls   and railings
and sometimes flowers
    (...?)   and rich
       flowers
    like poppies
I paint the sun   the different
        suns   I see

I paint the gable ends
of houses
through windows
canals and rivers
all these things
I try to give
the intensity of life to
the momentary
eternal
vividness
or delicacy
as best I can

Editorial note

The marks (...?) appear in this form in the manuscript, suggesting that the choice of word was still unresolved.

The Last Poem

During his final illness, Arthur Berry dictated his last poem from his hospital bed at North Staffordshire Royal Infirmary, Newcastle-under-Lyme.

The last poem is published here for the first time by kind permission of Cynthia Berry, to mark Arthur's centenary year.

It is possible that the cricket match of this final poem was Staffordshire vs Surrey playing in the Minors at The Oval on 22nd June 1994, twelve days before Arthur's death on 4th July. The outcome of this agonising match hung in the balance until the very last moments. Staffordshire eventually lost by 9 wickets, an especially stinging result given that one of the star performances on the Surrey side came from a player who had until recently played for Staffordshire.

How shall we say in this bed of nails
That a cricket ball delivered
At twenty-two yards
From wicket to wicket
Should hold the ecstasy of my world,
Between a few yards of Surrey Earth,
My heart.

Bibliography

Works by Arthur Berry

Books

A Three and Sevenpence Halfpenny Man, Kermase Editions (1986), autobiography
The Little Gold-Mine, Bullfinch Publications (1991), novel
The Tin Chapel, Barewall Books (2025), adapted for children

Poems

Poems by Arthur Berry, Graphic Design (Staffs) Ltd (1971)
Street Corner Ballads, Ironmarket Press (1977)
Dandelions, privately published (1993); North Staffordshire Press (2007 and 2015); Barewall Books (2025)
On The Street, Barewall Books (2018)

Plays

Commissioned and produced at the Victoria Theatre, Stoke-on-Trent:

The Spanish Dancer from Pinnox Street (1976)
Dr Fergo's Last Passion (1979)
Quiet Please (1981)
Dr Fergo Rides Again (1982)
The Sweet Bird of Card Street (1984)

Commissioned to open the New Vic Theatre:

St George of Scotia Road (1986)

Completed and produced at the New Vic Theatre to commemorate the centenary of Arthur Berry's birth:

Whatever Happened to Phoebe Salt? (2025)

Audio-visual

Lullaby of Queen Street (1979 on cassette tape); Barewall (2015 on CD)
Some Cinders, Some Dockweed, Barewall (2019 on CD)
A Bunch of Flowers, audio recording (c.1988) animated by Steve Redfearn with Barewall (2025)

A Three and Sevenpence Ha'penny Man: Arthur's TV Appearances, DVD, Staffordshire Film Archive (2015)
Arthur Berry: His Plays at the Victoria Theatre (Arthur at the Vic), DVD, Staffordshire Film Archive (2016)
Arthur Berry: An Observer of Urban Life, exhibition catalogue, Barewall Books (2015)

About Arthur Berry

Peter Davies, *Arthur Berry: A Ragged Richness*, Barewall Books (2022)

Biography

Arthur Berry was born in Smallthorne in 1925, the son of a colliery bricklayer and a publican's daughter. He was educated at Biddulph Council School, Burslem School of Art and The Royal College of Art (1943–46).

He taught at Manchester, Chelsea and Burslem Colleges of Art and was appointed Principal Lecturer in Painting at the North Staffordshire Polytechnic.

Arthur Berry had five plays commissioned and produced by the Victoria Theatre and was commissioned to write a play for the opening of the New Vic Theatre in 1986. He also wrote and recorded a series of monologues that were broadcast on BBC radio in the 1980s and 90s. His status as a Northern Artist of note was confirmed by a major exhibition of his paintings in 2015, hung alongside the work of L.S. Lowry. A critical appraisal of his work, *Arthur Berry: A Ragged Richness*, by Northern Art critic Peter Davies (Barewall Books, 2022), puts the work of Arthur Berry into context in relation to the European art movements of the mid-20th century.

Arthur Berry died on 4th July 1994.

His paintings continue to be exhibited regularly, and his work is held in public galleries and private collections around the world.

Acknowledgements

Thanks are due to the following for their support in producing this book:

The Estate of Arthur Berry
Cynthia Berry
The New Vic Theatre
The Victoria Theatre Archive
Arthur Berry 100 Project Team
Heritage Lottery Fund
Romy Cheeseman